THE ETERNAL NETWORK

THE ENDS
AND BECOMINGS OF
NETWORK CULTURE

EDITED BY
KRISTOFFER GANSING
AND INGA LUCHS

COLOPHON

The Eternal Network: The Ends and Becomings of Network Culture
Edited by Kristoffer Gansing and Inga Luchs

Authors: Clemens Apprich, Johanna Bruckner, Daphne Dragona, Kristoffer Gansing, Lorena Juan, Aay Liparoto, Geert Lovink, Alessandro Ludovico, Aymeric Mansoux, Rachel O'Dwyer, Luiza Prado de O. Martins, Roel Roscam Abbing, Femke Snelting, and Florian Wüst.

Editorial coordination: Tabea Hamperl
Copy-editing: Hannah Gregory and Rebecca Bligh
Cover design: The Laboratory of Manuel Bürger (Simon Schindele, Manuel Bürger)
Design & EPUB development: Barbara Dubbeldam
Publisher: Institute of Network Cultures, Amsterdam, and transmediale e.V., Berlin, 2020
ISBN print-on-demand: 978-94-92302-46-5
ISBN EPUB: 978-94-92302-45-8

Contact
Institute of Network Cultures - **Email**: info@networkcultures.org - **Web**: http://www.networkcultures.org

Order a copy or download this publication freely at http://networkcultures.org/publications. The publication is also available in German.

The Berlin-based transmediale festival publishes content related to its program in its online journal, of which this collection is an extension, published with the Institute of Network Cultures, Amsterdam. This edition is realized in the framework of transmediale 2020 *End to End* and its exhibition 'The Eternal Network', which takes place at Haus der Kulturen der Welt from 28 January – 1 March 2020. The exhibition is curated by Kristoffer Gansing with the advice of Clemens Apprich, Daphne Dragona, Geert Lovink, and Florian Wüst.

transmediale wishes to thank Geert Lovink and INC for their collaboration, and Miriam Rasch (INC) and Tabea Hamperl (transmediale) for the coordination of the overall project; Inga Luchs for her great co-editing, Hannah Gregory and Rebecca Bligh for their thorough copy-editing, and Jen Theodor for her patient work on the German translation. A heartfelt thanks goes out to all the authors who contributed to this volume.

transmediale has been funded as a cultural institution of excellence by Kulturstiftung des Bundes since 2004. For the wide range of supporters that help make each year's festival possible, visit transmediale. de/partners.

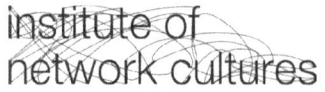

institute of
network cultures

transmediale/
art&
digitalculture

CONTENTS

INTRODUCTION

INTRODUCTION: NETWORK MEANS AND ENDS

KRISTOFFER GANSING

INTRODUCTION:
NETWORK MEANS AND ENDS

KRISTOFFER GANSING

The Persistent Ending of Networks

The internet has already ended many times – at least, it has when understood within the framework of network idealism, which, permeating the preceding century, has only 'heated up' over the past fifty years of globalization and the invention of the internet. 'The revolution is over. Welcome to the afterglow', was the curatorial tagline of transmediale 2014, formulated in light of the supposed wake-up call of Edward Snowden's revelations. A year later, *e-flux journal* published its anthology *The Internet Does Not Exist*, including, among others, Hito Steyerl's essay 'Too Much World: Is the Internet Dead?'.[1] This was back when the terms 'post-digital' and 'post-internet' were doing the rounds, both in critical media practice, and as a contemporary-art-world trend. Back then, the discussion was all about the internet becoming a fact of life, beyond the digital information exchange as such; impacting analog aesthetics, offline identities, ecologies, and geopolitics. Of course, the (virtual) reality of global financial networks (and their breakdowns) had already been reshaping life, politics, and networks of all scales, for a long time. Now, just as the financial sector remains largely obscure to the greater public, so, too, has the network culture that emerged along with the web, been subsumed within a larger framework of so-called digitalization characterized by platforms, opaque artificial intelligence, and largely invisible cloud infrastructures and services.

This is the age of platform and surveillance capitalism, in which, as Geert Lovink contends in his essay for this volume, nobody talks about networks anymore. The same fate seems to be slowly befalling the internet and the web. The latter, whose thirty-year anniversary was in March 2019, has come to be regarded as something as dreary as television, a view that has only intensified as the streaming model has claimed its dominance. According to Joel Waldfogel, consumers are now living through a new 'golden age' of the cultural industries.[2] Certainly, if we are to believe the statistics, global revenue from films, books, games, and music, has never been higher. If this *is* a golden age, then it is one not so much for the users, as, ironically, for those intermediaries that the network paradigm once promised to get rid of by means of decentralization and end-to-end communication.

---

1   Hito Steyerl, 'Too Much World: Is the Internet Dead?', in Julieta Aranda, Brian Kuan Wood, and Anton Vidokle (eds) *The Internet Does Not Exist*, Berlin: Sternberg Press, 2015, pp. 10-26.
2   Joel Waldfogel, 'How Digitization Has Created a Golden Age of Music, Movies, Books, and Television', *Journal of Economic Perspectives* 3 (Summer, 2017): 95-214.

Cut to 2019, when a call for conference papers announces 'The Ends of Social Media',[3] and when, whenever we hear about networks it is usually in the apocalyptic terms of network backlash: government-induced internet blackouts, fake news, botnets, trolls, and hate speech. How to reconcile the end of end-to-end — and, indeed, of liberal democracy — with this 'golden age' of media content, in which the personalized media revolution appears to have won out over the collective, and the network to have persisted, but become opaque, polarized, and anything but neutral? Maybe network idealism and the belief in net neutrality were misguided to start with? Now that the more tangible limits of networks are becoming visible, it might be time to readdress the network question, which is ultimately about future models of sociality, technology, and politics, in societies after globalization.

The Network is Everlasting

In 1967, Robert Filliou and George Brecht published a poem in which they stated that 'the network is everlasting'.[4] This was a piece of pre-internet culture, celebrating the interconnectedness of everyday lives and activities across an emerging global world, with specific relation to the authors' practice of mail art, using the postal system as a democratic means of communicational art-making. Filliou further developed a poetic imaginary of 'the eternal network', referring both to an existing network of post-avant-garde artist friends, and to 'the network' as an overarching metaphor for the organization of work and culture within this emerging world. As the art critic Lars Bang-Larsen has observed, before the network 'became dominated by digital connotations' it was 'a social concept'.[5] The starting point for this book (and accompanying exhibition) is a strategic reactivation of Filliou's notion of 'the eternal network', as an idea(l) of network culture beyond the technical reality of the actually existing one we know from our day-to-day online experience. From networks as idea(l), through the emergence and establishment of the internet and the subsequent network culture — in a way, closing a loop between pre- and post-internet reality.

In alignment with this perspective, the authors of this collection address the potentials and limits of networks, whether by reflecting on specific instances of critical network culture, and/or by suggesting new lines of thought and practice that might serve to replace or modify the network imaginary; whether referring to the multiple histories of networks, and/or going beyond networks in their current, established form(s). The book is an extension of the *End to End* transmediale 2020 festival in Berlin, which also features an exhibition entitled 'The Eternal Network'.

In the context of the vast contemporary technological, social, cultural, economic (and so forth), transformation known simply as 'digitalization', the book and exhibition ask what the current status of the network *is*. Here 'the network' implies both the paradigm of network idealism

3   Tero Karppi, 'CFP: The Ends of Social Media Symposium Nov 15 2019', The Ends of Social Media, 30
      May 2019, https://theendsofsocialmedia.home.blog/2019/05/30/the-ends/.
4   Georges Brecht and Robert Filliou, *Games at the Cedilla, or the Cedilla Takes Off*, New York: Something
      Else Press, 1967.
5   Lars Bang Larsen, *Networks*, Cambridge, MA: MIT Press, 2014, p. 13.

that emerged in the twentieth century – the network idea, as a positive, organizing social factor, if you will – as well as what could be called the 'actually existing' network culture that co-evolved with the technical network of the internet and the World Wide Web, during the 90s and beyond. The book and exhibition each attempt to explore the limits of networks, and of 'the network' – as, at once, a cultural and aesthetic imaginary, as well as a technological form – seeking forgotten and potential futures, with or without networks. Particular attention is paid to the legacies of a certain brand of critical internet and network culture that developed in Europe (and beyond) throughout the 90s, offering alternatives to the entrepreneurial ideals and solutionism of Silicon Valley.

From Networks to Networlds

The book's first section, 'Networks and Networlds', opens with Clemens Apprich's essay, 'The Never-ending Network', in which Deleuze and Guattari make a network-theory comeback; not in the form of their famous rhizome metaphor, but rather the idea of network logic producing eternal repetitions of the same. Rather than adopting a static model of sameness, however, Apprich argues that there is a capitalization of the difference-through-repetition of networked subjectivity, in how it constantly translates into the lucrative data points of platforms. For Apprich, there is a performative dimension to this algorithmic play of the same and the different which opens up the possibility of open-ended and never-ending networks, and, with it, of a new politics. In her contribution, 'Networks and Life-worlds', Daphne Dragona turns to the 'ends' of networks from another point of view, relating network nodes to the world-ending potential of the climate crisis. Pointing to the information networks that have enabled the perception and knowledge of this immanent ending, Dragona critically scrutinizes the networked sensory technologies and ideas that helped bring into being a systems-theory view of the Earth and of ecology in the first place. Similar to Apprich, Dragona does not end on a pessimistic note, instead discussing the potential reconfiguration of constructive network practices, while remaining aware of the limitations and pitfalls of cybernetic rationalism. In a survey of four interventionist art and design projects, Dragona sketches out new positions, queering common narratives about the Earth's systems, the biases of machine learning, and geoengineering, in ways that make room for more-than-human existence on a planetary scale.

Following this turn toward the field of ecological systems theory as an offshoot of cybernetic network principles, the artist and designer Luiza Prado de O. Martins' contribution, 'There Are Words and Worlds That Are Truthful and True' goes deeper into the despair and the politics of the environmental crisis. Recounting a research trip to her native Brazil, she describes meeting with marginalized communities within the framework of attempting to establish what she calls 'The Councils of the Pluriversal'. Instead of formal meetings with fixed protocols, these councils mutated into more fluid states of encounter between people, (failing) ecosystems, and Indigenous thinking, aesthetics, and, most importantly, local food ingredients. Here, cooking became the main medium for reflecting on shared and different ancestries and histories, as a means to connect and disconnect oppressive politics of identity and reproduction with climate change and its precarious and increasingly dangerous life-situations. In this way, the totalizing model of the universal network gives way to something else: community and communications, conducted according to the acknowledged existence of multiple realities, and the urgent need to decolonize knowledge cultures.

Human, Nonhuman, and Networks in Between

The essay 'Network Topologies: From the Early Web to Human Mesh Networks', by Alessandro Ludovico, opens the second section of the book, devoted to the 'Human, Nonhuman, and Networks In Between'. In his account of the independent publishing network associated with his long-running magazine, *Neural*, Ludovico highlights the changing topologies that have informed our understanding of the net and networked cultural production. Here again pre-internet mail-art networks come into the picture, as important reference points for the creation of web-based independent distribution infrastructures that were similarly playful and collaborative in nature. Tracing these changing network topologies, from mail art to net art, to today's data-driven platforms, Ludovico calls for a new movement of interdependent human-mesh networks, resisting the drive toward ever-more separated network identities.

A persistent belief in (or return to?) alternative networks also informs Rachel O'Dwyer's piece, 'Another Net Is Possible', which at the same time keeps a close tab on the now clear limitations of pirate utopias, on- and offline. Analyzing community wireless networks within a wider history of activists claiming the electromagnetic spectrum as a commons, O'Dwyer sketches out the attendant drawbacks of such movements' attempts to overcome the neoliberal order, finding them to display uncannily common characteristics including technofetishism, 'open' and collaborative structures that are not so open or equal in practice, and a drive always to scale up. Against these aspects of activist networks, O'Dwyer pits practices of 'inventive materiality', such as Etherpunk's use of FM radio spectrum infrastructures for low-tech internet communication. Such networks and their practitioners recognize their limitations, she argues, regarding as strengths, instead of weaknesses, the finite, local and messy nature of their interactions.

In the piece that follows, the focus of the conversation between Aay Liparoto and Lorena Juan is a network project that, in a very conscious way, works with the strengths of its own limitations. In 'Everything We Build', they discuss the collaborative practice of the queer-feminist wiki platform *Not Found On*, which Liparoto initiated in 2019. The platform constitutes a rethinking, from an intersectional perspective, of the way that collective and open-source projects and knowledge resources are conducted and cared for. Offering a web service that is closed to the general public, Liparoto and their collaborators attempt to create the online equivalent of a 'safe space', for individuals (or dividuals) and communities that, due to their precarious social status, do not necessarily want to be exposed on so-called open and participatory mainstream platforms. Recalling Flavia Dzodan's cry, 'My feminism will be intersectional or it will be bullshit!',[6] it is possible to see this project as a modification of earlier cyberfeminist practices, adapting them to a post-digital public reality which is characterized both by higher LGBTQIA+ visibility, and an alarming rise in hate speech and hate crimes in the wake of right-wing politics.

---

6   Flavia Dzodan, 'My feminism will be intersectional or it will be bullshit!', *Tiger Beatdown*, 10 October 2011, http://tigerbeatdown.com/2011/10/10/my-feminism-will-be-intersectional-or-it-will-be-bullshit/.

Closing off this section, Johanna Bruckner's text, 'Molecular Sex and Polymorphic Sensibilities', is a speculative proposal for new types of interspecies sexuality and subjectivity that could take us beyond oppressive binaries. Just as quantum computing promises a world of networks in which ones and zeroes simultaneously coexist with one another, Bruckner's artwork describes a fictive future sexbot that is seemingly able to freely mutate from one state of being to another. Taking its cue from a sea creature called the 'brittle star', this bot is a portrait of social, technological, and bio-chemical entanglements, as they exist in (non)human networks, after the impact of phenomena such as micro-plastics. Following the writings of Karen Barad, the project asks how the molecularization and indeterminacy of being, today, might inform queer and hybrid futures better tooled to deal with current technological, political and ecological changes.

Endings and New Becomings

In the final section, 'Endings and New Becomings', Geert Lovink offers an impassioned 'Requiem for the Network', reflecting on the possible death not only of network culture, but also the particular brand of critical and autonomous net cultures for which he himself helped to advocate from the mid-1990s onwards. As is fitting, he doesn't stay with the nostalgic resentment of the aging internet critic: instead, by introducing interviews, he turns the piece into a conversation with multiple networked voices, offering up further perspectives on the fate of networks in the age of platforms. By the end, it is clear that not everything has been said on 'the network question'. Lovink is still hopeful for the prospects of organized networks, and for further outgrowths of network culture, beyond the 'smart' and online boredom, into worlds where tech, human, and nonhuman infrastructures are necessarily 'contaminated' by one another, not least on the affective plane. Femke Snelting's piece, 'Other Geometries', is another piece of autocriticism written after the author's participation in a 2018–19 transmediale Study Circle on the topic of 'Affective Infrastructures'. Reflecting on the collective work with which this interdisciplinary circle was initially tasked, Snelting points to the limitations of circular sociality for creating a dynamic infrastructure for collective work. She goes on to address the limitations of node-based models of distributed networks which have their foundation in Cold War-era notions of 'creating resilience', arguing that, today, it is necessary to pay greater attention to what happens *between* the nodes, and to create less normative infrastructures. With reference to Zach Blas's notion of the 'paranodal', as well as Anna Lowenhaupt Tsing's work with fungal infrastructures as inspiration for geometries of relations beyond the calculative, Snelting recalls that the study group was asked the question of how to concretize and turn such geometries into 'actual tools and software'. The hesitant answer, according to Snelting, was that these could only be both complex and concrete.

This neatly leads us to the final contribution of the volume: 'Seven Theses on the Fediverse and the Becoming of FLOSS', by Aymeric Mansoux and Roel Roscam Abbing. This is a thorough discussion of one of the most significant developments in alternative network cultures of recent years, reflecting many aspects of all that is discussed within the volume, including questions of selective online presence, precarious communities, platform independent and co-developed platform infrastructures, and environmental sustainability. The authors discuss how, in what they call the 'latest episode of the never-ending saga of net and computational culture', the emergence of federated network initiatives is challenging the established working methodologies of FLOSS (Free/Libre and Open-Source Software). For Mansoux and Roscam Abbing, this opens up new ways to accomplish crucial links between independent media and the structures of owning, building, and maintaining networks.

'Digitalization' – Sounds Like a 90s Party

It might seem a bit retro to be taking up the discussion of networks today, as something more properly belonging to the 90s along with Manuel Castell's thesis on *The Rise of the Network Society*,[7] actor-network theory, films such as *The Matrix*, and of course the mass popularization of the internet through the World Wide Web. Today, even within the larger contemporary debate on digitalization, networks have come to figure as a hidden technical layer, rather than as something whose discussion is, in itself, a cultural force. Meanwhile, however, many other buzzwords and phenomena of thirty years or so ago are now re-emerging, into what could well be called digitalization's normative phase. In many ways, the 90s are back, or so it seems – only look at the kind of topics that are at the forefront of today's digital culture. Virtual reality, immersion, artificial intelligence: all as present as they were in the early multimedia years of the 90s, and again in the new millennium's first five years of 'new media' hype. Of course, this time around, there are differences in how those terms are used and understood, as well as in the technical realities behind them. The German media theorist Friedrich Kittler once famously wrote that 'the media age proceeds in jerks, like Turing's paper strip.'[8] From today's post-digital standpoint, it seems rather to proceed in parallel loops in which the past continuously makes comebacks. What's more, it seems these loops are often slightly skewed, offering up some strange returns.

Network Backlash and The Old New Outside

If 'the network' is interesting, it is precisely as something slightly out of tune with these other loops, as a forgotten component of digitalization in the post-digital phase of the digital's becoming infrastructural. If we turn to the internet, its being hyped as a thing-in-itself seems to have receded in favor of its being positioned more as an infrastructural backbone for data-dependent services, and a delivery platform for the streaming economy. Now, when 'the internet' and 'networks' appear in discussions of the consequences of digitalization, it is often in the context of the previously mentioned backlash against net culture. The internet sociologist Yochai Benkler's reformulation of 'the wealth of nations' as 'the wealth of networks'[9] has transformed into 'the poverty of networks',[10] as it is now the limits, rather than the endless and universal possibilities of networks, that are most tangible.

7   Manuel Castells, *The Rise of the Network Society*, Malden, MA: Blackwell, 1996.
8   Friedrich Kittler, *Gramophone, Film, Typewriter*, trans. Geoffrey Winthrop-Young and Michael Wutz, Stanford: Stanford University Press, 1999, p. 18.
9   Yochai Benkler, *The Wealth of Networks: How Social Production Transforms Markets and Freedom*, New Haven: Yale University Press, 2006.
10   David Berry, 'The Poverty of Networks', *Theory, Culture & Society* 7-8 (December, 2008): 364-372.

Arguably a defining moment for the network generation was when, twenty years ago, Michael Hardt and Antonio Negri stated in *Empire* that there was no longer any outside, and that all resistance now came from within, postulating the multitude as a form of disruptive counter-power of many particulars.[11] Ironically, the actual rise of 'the network society' could well be defined in terms of the many battles waged against perceived 'outsiders' (who themselves often take on networked forms) – from the 'war on terror' with its 'axis of evil', to the so-called refugee crisis. Take, even, the marginalized 'losers' left out of today's neoliberal democracies, victims of the 'downward mobility' that is now a core component of digital societies,[12] who are politically mobilized through social media networks.

In spite of the toxicity, virality and resentment of many such movements, don't they actually point to the potential of networks to generate outsides? Rather than lament the fall of Western liberalism and deliberative democracy, might we not, instead, actuate this potential for new social organization, both in and beyond networks, claiming the new, post-representational politics to which it caters for socially progressive forces? For the intersectional left, this would mean engaging more actively with networks, taking into account their now-more-tangible limits. This returns to what is meant, within this project, by discussing the limit to networks – as a kind of mapping of what network culture once was, and what it may or may not become, toward reforming as well as refuting the same. The strange return of 'the network': not, any longer, as the answer to everything, but as a specific option within a new post-digital political landscape.

The transmediale 2020 festival *End to End* and its accompanying exhibition 'The Eternal Network' open-endedly explore this strange return, even via exiting networks and imagining alternatives, such as new internet infrastructures; queering networks, decolonizing networks, catering to different scales of organization and sociopolitical urgencies, and rejuvenating DIY practices. This volume also reflects on some of the histories and legacies of the network, discussing critical shifts and dis/continuities in order to reorient our understanding and undertaking of critical network cultures in the present.

11   Michael Hardt and Antonio Negri, *Empire*, Cambridge: Harvard University Press, 2000.
12   Oliver Nachtwey, *Germany's Hidden Crisis. Social Decline in the Heart of Europe*, London: Verso, 2018.

WHAT WAS THE NETWORK?

CLEMENS APPRICH, DAPHNE DRAGONA, GEERT LOVINK, AND FLORIAN WÜST

CONVERSATION MODERATED BY KRISTOFFER GANSING

WHAT WAS THE NETWORK?

A Conversation on the Possibilities and Limits of the Network Imaginary

CLEMENS APPRICH, DAPHNE DRAGONA, GEERT LOVINK, AND FLORIAN WÜST - *CONVERSATION MODERATED BY KRISTOFFER GANSING*

On August 6, 2019, the curatorial advisors of the transmediale 2020 exhibition, 'The Eternal Network', gathered at the festival's offices in Berlin for a conversation on the status of network culture and theory today. Starting from the question 'What was the network?', the conversation explored the multiple trajectories of networks within cybernetics, art and philosophy, also taking the limits of networks into account. This included a reconsideration of the role of alternative and critical networks in today's widespread digitalization, with its data-centric platform economy and the techno-cultural changes wrought by artificial intelligence.

Kristoffer Gansing: The first question I would like to address is: 'What was the network?' With this we can also think about whether we are in a moment in which it is possible to historicize networks, and if so, why we would do that.

Florian Wüst: What I find quite provocative is the past tense: 'What *was* the network?' In the discourse around the digital, we have indeed moved somewhere else under the conditions of surveillance capitalism and platforms. We are in a totally different situation compared to what we historically refer to as the networks of the 90s, when there was big hope for a functioning decentralization of information and agency. But if I look at other fields, I have the feeling that networks haven't even been built, so how could they have dissolved? Areas where people haven't yet managed to come together for joint action beyond small groups or neighborhoods. Take for example the many urban grassroots initiatives in Berlin, which are only recently making efforts to create larger networks in order to fight gentrification. I think there is an interesting gap between how in digital culture and theory there is the perception that we are beyond something, that the network has already been lost or corrupted, and how in other fields, in practice, we are only beginning to reach the next stages of networked collaboration and communication.

Daphne Dragona: When I first read the question, 'What was the network?', I thought rather of the architectural topology that was not realized, the dream of the decentralized or even distributed architecture of the network, that didn't come into being. The dream of a network that was in reality taken over by the more sovereign and mainstream infrastructures. And now there is this question that always takes me back to the expectations of the 90s, and the first platforms – IRC, Usenet. All these expectations were there – so what happened, what changed? The approach of Manuel Castells, for example, was all about how communication networks would bring change to society, politics, economy, and culture. And this change did happen, but not how it had been imagined. Now we also see the dark sides of the network.

On a personal level, when I think back to the late 90s, early 00s, I still remember how important it was that connectivity had come along. I was in Athens at that time, working for a festival of art and new technologies, as we described them then, Medi@terra. At first the festival was Greek, then it expanded to include the Balkans, and then became international. The festival grew thanks to the networks that we built with other festivals and centers in the field, thanks to the research we could do online and to the interest that audiences and funding bodies showed in the emergence of digital networks. For me, the network was this potentiality. But now it doesn't seem so possible to believe in any longer.

Geert Lovink: Let's talk about the network question. My essay is titled 'Requiem for the Network' but the working title was 'Network Renaissance'. As you can see, I am in two minds: Will the network vanish or reappear? There's a certain reluctance of a particular generation (maybe my generation and the generation that followed) to write our political media history in the same way as the 1968 generation wrote theirs. There used to be a collective obligation to write one's history in order to pass it on to the next generation but I don't see that really happening at the moment. It's not something that seems to come naturally any longer. Maybe due to doubt about the concept of History itself. Instead of reassessing the history-in-the-making of our networks, movements, communities, and events, digging into memories and recounting anecdotes, we tend to reflect on the concept itself.

Clemens Apprich: In media studies we love these kinds of past-tense questions. However, the current debate about digitalization seems to be completely ahistorical, as though the 'digital' had only just entered the stage. This historical oblivion is particularly true when it comes to networks and their implementation in digital media industries. Yet reflecting on the past doesn't necessarily imply outdated historicism, in the sense of understanding a specific time in history that leads straight to the present. What I'm interested in is media genealogy, which is nonlinear and eclectic. Walter Benjamin calls this 'historicity', in contrast to historicism, or '*Jetztzeit*' ('here-and-now') – a term that perfectly fits the 'eternal present' of this year's exhibition, 'The Eternal Network'. What he means by this is that two widely disparate historical events may have more in common than two events close together in time. This historicity is ever-present, aligning the past with the here and now – and so also with the future. What Daphne said about the looming dream of the network and its potentiality for today is a good depiction of such a *Jetztzeit*.

KG: Is there potential for a strange return of the network within digitalization or is this just the nostalgic projection of a previous network generation? Or, even with a hint of such nostalgia, could there still be value in this idea vis-à-vis how digitalization has become the new catch-all term, and seems to operate on an even vaster scale than the network did or does.

CA: When we talk about digitalization, we are of course talking about a decades- or even centuries-old development. But we don't have to go through the whole history in order to reflect on it. Making the present intelligible through past events can be very episodic. This is also an interesting point about the network metaphor – that it has this untimeliness to it. It pops up in the 90s to make sense of quite different socioeconomic developments, such as a new worldwide communication infrastructure with the hope for democratic expression and the latest push toward a fully globalized capitalism. With this, the network becomes an all-encompassing, all-explaining concept, from food chains to supply industries to nervous systems. Patrick Jagoda has called this the 'network sublime': the network is everything and nothing.[1] And maybe that's the best thing that could have happened to it – to become this weird and untimely concept. Like *Jetztzeit*, it can always actualize, it can connect to different types of pasts and futures.

And the fascinating thing in today's context is that this 'becoming a network' or 'network-becoming' is also about becoming invisible. Most recent debates about digitalization tend to be dominated by debates about platforms. But it is still the network, at least from my perspective, that is the driving force – the motor – behind most of digital culture's phenomena. Even though digital capitalism has solidified into platforms over the last decade, the inner working of these platforms, the way they produce value via data extraction and interpretation is still based on a network logic.

GL: It might be interesting to look at this problem from the perspective of contemporary art. In the field of contemporary art in the 90s, the network played an important role. Maybe it wasn't that technological, or focused on the internet per se, but it was still very present. Cities, institutions, scenes, and groups were in constant communication and comparison with each other: Frankfurt, Köln, London, New York, Berlin… What Daphne said about Athens is a typical example. Whether those networks were internet-driven or not wasn't the main issue. How then do we look at the reluctance to write history from that perspective?

KG: Maybe this also has something to do with the inherently anti-narrative stream of thinking within new media and network theory, where linear representation is not an important issue. What was usually on its main agenda was how you acted or performed in a given project, rather than how you narrated it. The reluctance to write this history therefore also comes from the kind of anti-representational thinking inherent to working with and within networks, and the wish for forms immanent to the form itself.

DD: But why do you think that we need to write this history in the first place? Once you write the book, you capture, generalize, Westernize. Who would be the ones to write that history, and why? Who and what would be left out? There is always an issue between the topographies and the topologies of networks. The locations considered to be important on the map end up defining the strong nodes of the network.

KG: I think that this also relates to the question of what we can actually learn from these histories of 'Critical Internet Cultures', and relatedly, what the blind spots of the contemporary moment are with respect to this question. Clemens for instance co-edited a book about 'forgotten futures',[2] pointing to the idea that we should perhaps also consider net cultures that never happened or were never heard about. This prompts another question as to the limits of networks.

---

1   See, for instance, Patrick Jagoda, *Network Aesthetics*, Chicago: The University of Chicago Press, 2016.
2   Clemens Apprich and Felix Stalder (eds), *Vergessene Zukunft. Radikale Netzkulturen in Europa*, Bielefeld: transcript Verlag, 2012.

CA: Yes, but the problem remains even with speculative accounts about *the* history of networks. Any history changes with your location and your point of view. It's interesting to see, for example, how the network has been discussed and theorized in Latin America. '*La red*', rather than 'network', evokes a vastly different understanding and imaginary about what a connection is. The work of Tania Pérez-Bustos, an anthropologist from Bogotá, describes how this term [which translates to 'the web' in English] correlates with techniques of weaving, a performative act.[3] Such an understanding sparks an alternate history of the network with all its untold and unrealized threads that we are trying to weave together here. I guess in the end we are all caught up in our own network histories with their idiosyncrasies and blind spots.

DD: It depends how you see it. In the past there was a lot of discussion about networks being 'walled gardens'. One could say that what lies beyond one's network is difference, because networks are based on sameness. Other worlds, opinions, and realities are kept away from you. Networks are not porous. They are vulnerable, as Geert has discussed elsewhere, but they are not porous; you cannot easily break through them.

FW: It's the same with the term 'community'. There is something exclusive about it, when it should rather be inclusive. In his theory of the urban commons, Greek author and activist Stavros Stavrides problematizes the often privatized or gated character of communities. Without the distribution of power, commoning quickly becomes enclosure, Stavrides argues.[4] He instead advocates for common spaces that aren't defined by boundaries and that remain open for newcomers. Such processes require radically new social relations, based on equality and solidarity. Stavrides talks primarily about the urban environment as well as social practice, both of which expand into digital space, or vice versa, are increasingly organized by and in interaction with digital infrastructures.

CA: Thinking about the limits of networks and what lies beyond them, I am made to think of the system, which, somehow, was the first victim of the network. Before the 90s, the 'system' not the network was the dominant concept to describe society. However, with an increasingly globalized and networked world, the idea of social groups, institutions, and even the nation state as contained systems broke up. The system began to leak, and opened up into myriads of networks. For some this had a liberating effect, but it also created problems. Beyond a network is always another network. As Wendy Chun says, the network is such a compelling concept, because with it, or better within it, you are always searching and never finding.[5] You constantly zoom in and zoom out, switching from one network to another. The network gives you the opportunity or even the excuse not to make a decision, not to define an inside and outside, not to look for an exit. You are trapped within the network.

3   Discussion during a workshp in Bogotá, Colombia in February 2015. For a report of the workshop see: Sara Morais dos Santos Bruss, 'Making Change – A Report from Bogotá', *spheres – Journal for Digital Cultures* 2 (2015), http://spheres-journal.org/making-change-a-report-from-bogota/.

4   See, for instance, Stavros Stavrides, *Common Space. The City as Commons*, Chicago, IL: University of Chicago Press, 2016 and Stavros Stavrides, *Common Spaces of Urban Emancipation*, Manchester, UK: Manchester University Press, 2019.

5   Wendy Chun, *Updating to Remain the Same*, Cambridge, MA: MIT Press, 2016, p. 29ff.

Yet as Deleuze and Guattari demonstrated, every repetition has the potential of difference – for bifurcation. The things that seem to be especially repetitive are those that have the most potential to produce something new. What I like about this idea is that bifurcations happen all the time. This is what I'm trying to get at in my essay for this volume: that the network still has this potential; that it can connect different times and places. I want to argue against a reticular pessimism – that is, the idea that everything is trapped and captured within a network. You simply cannot capture everything.

KG: That difference may always be generated is an important point but there might be a trap within this Deleuzian perspective in terms of its politics. I'm thinking about the hard edges of networks, in terms of class, race, gender, and their related issues, which are so tangible today. Despite the use of networked, supposedly horizontal social media, exclusions have far from disappeared. Everybody is on the platform, but it became a tribalized space. I guess this is a question about practice and possibility – of what, ultimately, is at stake in the network question today?

CA: The idea is precisely not to hide nor dissolve political categories, such as class, race, and gender, in some kind of network sublimity, but to make the edges visible and tangible, in order to enable bifurcations.

GL: I still think in mass psychological terms that the network is one of many possible ways to organize the social. In the same way as there are cells, groups, tribes, communities, unions, and political parties. Maybe this list will change and grow in the decades to come. Maybe some forms of social organization will return. Shall we envision and design new forms of the social that have not yet existed, rather than referring to the old forms we are familiar with?

From Social to Neural, with and Beyond Networks

DD: It is also important to consider what the dominant model of a network is for each era. Today, discussion has shifted to the area of artificial intelligence, with the dominant model being the artificial neural network. This brings us to topologies that are much more complicated, much more opaque, compared to the informational and social ones we have met up to now, even if all of these somehow intersect. I feel that this affects the discourse on networks, for example when we are talking about the Smart Home or the Smart City. Because these environments, the environments that we live in, are being adapted based on how these machines operate; how these machines see, read, and sense the world.

CA: The field of network analytics, which is the driving force behind most of today's applications in AI and machine learning, actually predefines how we see the world, how things are filtered for us, and also how the world sees us. Think about recommendation systems, which follow a very crude network logic that tells you what you should like is what others like you like, or that the friend of your friend should also be your friend. This leads to the much-discussed filter bubbles and echo chambers. But it doesn't have to be that way, we are not talking about a natural law. We could come up with different network logics. The problem with the dominant one is that it has become invisible and therefore acts as if it is indeed natural.

DD: The invisibility of the network is also what made us stop referring to it in a way. That's a bit like what Wendy Chun discusses in her book, *Updating to Remain the Same: Habitual New Media*. The less we see or pay attention to networks or technologies, the less we name them and reflect upon them. But that doesn't mean that networks do not play a significant role. Actually, they play an even more significant role as we become the machines or the networks. They define our daily lives and habits.

CA: Exactly. The network has become so pervasive that everyone follows its logic. But how many people actually know about TCP/IP or other internet protocols, for example? Even in media studies I would say that the majority of scholars do not know how the internet works, let alone how it came into being. Just because it works, shouldn't stop us from critically reflecting on it. Here a media genealogical understanding might be advantageous.

GL: In the late 90s network theory turned into network science, and then stopped. I am not saying that people have stopped thinking about networks but this specific trajectory stalled. Castells's network society has not been widely adopted. Lately I've been in contact with some people in the European Commission in Brussels who are fierce promoters of network science. I challenged them to prove whether this science is alive and has any relevance. What has it produced lately? There's a desire to bring scientists on board. The whole world of social networks has become so dark, fluffy, and messy to them that they felt they needed to bring scientists back on board to get rid of all the myths once and for all – the commercial interests and the hidden forces. In this view the network is a mysterious invisible power that produces fake news and then produces conspiracies.

In the social sciences more and more people say that we need to introduce technical solutions, because according to them, our understanding of society has completely failed. But we are already caught in a complex kind of technical, bureaucratic society: this is our reality. So this limiting of the horizon, it's quite real. It does not open up discussions about alternatives at all. I wish there was another type of network theory that could now thrive. Then, the discussion around this table would be very different. What would have happened if decentralized networks would have been programmed to resist any form of centralization?

KG: This relates to what I asked about the limits of networks. What you describe is one limit, concerning just one particular way of dealing with or thinking about networks. Couldn't we say that actually the limits of network science, as with many other models of networks, are linked with this typical image of the network lines and nodes, which constitutes a flat ontology, where on the one hand everything is possible, but on the other everything is traced and mapped. When we talk about invisibility, it seems like we are talking not about the usual question of scale, but about a kind of multiversal thinking, which is actually often lacking in network thinking, especially as we move into the age of AI based on deep learning and neural networks. Fake news, propaganda, and so on, they all, in their banality, point to many hidden networks that are operating at the same time in order to produce the general network effect. This multiversal operation is what makes new network science extremely successful within, for example, the manipulation of the election process in the US.

CA: An interesting and somehow built-in 'limit' of the network in relation to AI and machine learning lies in the very beginning of cybernetics. As Orit Halpern has discussed, the cybernetic vision of Warren McCulloch and Walter Pitts, who theorized the possibility of an artificial neural network in 1943, led them to a computational rationality, which was no longer based on reason.[6] As a consequence, the network, in their view, turns psychotic; it leads to an overproduction of meaning, an unreasonable situation in which any form of symbolic closure is no longer relevant. This is the situation we find ourselves in today: artificial neural networks promote a hyper-inductive approach and, at the same time, dump the idea of symbolic reasoning. Just look into the data and the rest will follow. But it's still people who build these models, and inevitably, they implement their very specific and biased understanding of what they want to do with the data. You can't just dissolve this symbolic baggage in a supposedly flat ontology or hide it in network scientific discourse – as psychoanalysis has shown over and over again, every time you try to repress the symbolic, it reemerges somewhere else. So it comes as no surprise if artificial neural networks discriminate along the lines of a socially, that is symbolically unjust system. They are not so unreasonable after all, but follow the biases we produce as a society.

GL: This genre of scientific approach does dominate, even though it itself is invisible. This approach is not talked about, it is just translated into software interfaces, APIs, you name it. And then millions or billions of people are confronted with by them. But the thing itself is outside of the frame, and maybe it is necessary to remind everybody that the hard network science approach is extremely successful. It hasn't moved on conceptually, and has categorically refused to face other neighboring approaches. And it is in the full swing of implementation. That's why many people may be reluctant to say the network is dead because it's so obviously not.

CA: Yes, that's exactly the point. I would just disagree on one point: I don't think that these network models are out of reach; they are not black-boxed, as is often claimed to be the case. If you want to know more about neural networks or machine learning methods, you can, for example, download and use Google's TensorFlow platform. Of course, you might object that this in itself is a technical framework, that for most people it is still out of reach. But for people in media studies, the arts, or activism, who want to engage with these debates, I don't see why they shouldn't take a crash course in machine learning offered by Google.

DD: We can go on having the discussion around the black-boxing of technology forever. I think this is a multifaceted issue. It depends on what exactly we are discussing. When you buy a product that is based on AI, they won't tell you how exactly it operates based on voice recognition and how it will be used by advertisers. The term black-boxing is still prevalent, because users once again don't know what is happening with their data. At least that's how I understand it, in the case of devices like Alexa. I was reading recently that Alexa will be used to perform health care tasks. Will the user be informed about how their health-related data will be used and by whom?

---

6   Orit Halpern, *Beautiful Data: A History of Vision and Reason since 1945*, Durham, NC: Duke University Press, 2015.

CA: I think, Alexa, Siri, or Google Assistant are good examples for extending the notion of the black box. After all, when it was conceptualized in cybernetics, it didn't mean that we shouldn't touch it. On the contrary, the black box was introduced as a methodological tool in order to experiment with complex systems. So why not experiment with Alexa, Siri, and co.? This can happen on a technical, as well as on an artistic, theoretical, or even legal level. We should get our hands dirty if we want to formulate a critique of these systems.

DD: Maybe we need to consider the role of algorithmic decision-making and automation in relation to human decision-making. When it comes to social networks or cultural networks or how we work together, it's basically up to us to what extent we are able to build networks where we acknowledge the importance of difference and escape the creation of closed worlds.

KG: There is a suggestion by Tiziana Terranova, quoted in your text, Geert, of shifting the idea of connectionism from our present model to quantum entanglement. It's a very speculative proposal where she is saying that this could also produce 'spooky' results.

GL: You can see here that networks are based on uncanny experiences. They become centralized through the endless production of sameness. Certain dating apps play with that. Most of them produce a boring repetition of sameness: you provide the apps with your specifications and it will look for matches. But there are other logics. For instance, in the very beginning, during the brief period of locative media, people would encounter others purely based on location. And because of this, matching became much more random. That's what I thought of when Terranova spoke of 'spooky' results. The eternal return of the same can be broken up.

NETWORKS AND
NETWORLDS

THE NEVER-ENDING NETWORK: A REPETITIVE AND (THUS) DIFFERENTIATING CONCEPT OF OUR TIME

CLEMENS APPRICH

THE NEVER-ENDING NETWORK: A REPETITIVE AND (THUS) DIFFERENTIATING CONCEPT OF OUR TIME

CLEMENS APPRICH

I.

Is a network centralized, decentralized, or distributed?[1] May it even be a scale-free network?[2] The question of what exactly a network is birthed a new research area at the interface of mathematics – in particular graph theory and statistics – biology, chemistry, computer science, psychology, physics, and sociology. Network science, as this area was called, deals with complex networks, such as food webs, electric grids, transport systems, neural circuits, computer or social nets, by dissecting real-world phenomena into abstract representations of nodes and links. Representing biological, physical, and social realities in network terms has the objective to build predictive models and extrapolate future behavior from past and existing data. In this way, networks provide orientation in an increasingly complex world, and, by virtue of their explanatory power, have arguably become the universal concept of our time.[3] They are depictions, figurations, and projections at the same time. They are, in an odd way, that which is depicted, and that which makes the depiction possible. Networks are signifiers in a world that has been described as being without signification.[4] Given this postmodern paradox, we might be better off asking not what a network is, thus getting caught in an endless chain of representations, but rather understanding the network's causes and effects. Following Gilles Deleuze, we might ask: What brings the network into the world, both in terms of the enabling conditions for this all-encompassing concept and the actual formation of the network as a specific expression of the time we live in?[5] It has become a truism to say that we live in a networked world, and it is more and more difficult to imagine a world outside the network. However, the eternal return in network form, which can feel like an endless repetition of the same, also suggests the possibility of difference. In this essay, I will look into this possibility with regard to digital media networks by contrasting them with recent debates about the epistemic impossibility of accessing the world – networked or not.[6]

1   Paul Baran, 'On Distributed Communications', *RAND* (1964), https://www.rand.org/pubs/research_memoranda/RM3420.html.

2   Albert-László Barabási and Eric Bonabeau, 'Scale-Free Networks', *Scientific American* 288 (2003): 50-59.

3   Wendy Hui Kyong Chun, *Updating to Remain the Same. Habitual New Media*, Cambridge: MIT Press, 2016, pp. 39ff.

4   Fredric Jameson, *Postmodernism, or The Cultural Logic of Late Capitalism*, Durham: Duke University Press, 1991.

5   Gilles Deleuze, *Difference and Repetition*, trans. Paul Patton, New York: Columbia University Press, 1994 (1968), in particular the introduction.

6   My thanks go to Thomas Lamarre for an inspiring conversation on this subject.

Let me start by making some fairly obvious observations, in order to clear the way. Firstly, networks have no beginning or end. Each node within a network may be an intersection to another network. Hence, a linear understanding of a network is impossible, because it cannot encompass all of a network's possible forms. To think about network forms as means of social, economic, or cultural expression necessitates a critical reflection of the respective desires that have spawned these very forms. For example, random networks are a direct expression of a mathematical desire for an absolute form,[7] whereas scale-free networks actualize the empirical complexity of social, but also biological, physical, and other realities.[8] Secondly, networks evolve over time. Instead of trying to essentialize a specific network form by making it the standard for all other forms, it is more insightful to evaluate its genealogy.[9] The invention of a worldwide computer network, for instance, was not a singular act of history. Rather, the emergence of the internet involved a historical folding as a combination of heterogeneous and opposing vectors, from technical developments (e.g. TCP/IP versus OSI-standard), to institutional frameworks (e.g. ARPANET, NSFNET, Minitel), to social and individual practices (e.g. within Usenet and hacker cultures, or the first Bulletin Board Systems). Here the idea of random networks laid the imaginary ground for their later implementation as a technology of decentralization and redistribution. Thirdly, networks follow certain rules. They may be virtually limitless, in the sense that they can morph into almost every form, but they are nonetheless limited in their actual formation. According to Alexander Galloway, a computer network relies on certain protocols, which specify how the network operates.[10] By setting the rules for the transmission of data from one computer to another, from one application to another, but also from one user to another, protocols steer and control possible behavior within a network such as the internet.

A protocol-based network has little in common with the still prevalent idea of an uncontrolled, anarchic space of data flows. However, such a network imaginary creates expectations of what a network can or should do. It influences decisions about the actual form and implementation of networks, and, similar to protocols, how the implemented network shapes and structures the world. In this sense, Galloway's focus on protocological control is somehow misleading. Certainly, the material basis of what we call the internet — which in its basic functioning is a top-level network that connects a series of sub-networks — consists of a range of protocols, summarized in the internet protocol suite. But the model entails more than TCP/IP — that is the Transmission Control Protocol (TCP), which runs on top of the Internet Protocol (IP), and already has 'control' in its name. Even though TCP/IP are foundational protocols in the suite, which make it possible to break up large data sets into smaller packages so

---

7   Paul Erdős and Alfréd Rényi, 'On Random Graphs', *Publicationes Mathematicae Debrecen* 6 (1959): 290-297. It is important to notice that the Erdős-Rényi model saw the application of random networks, which are defined by equally distributed nodes, as purely mathematical. Hence, the authors do not claim that their model has any explanatory use in the social or biological world.

8   Albert-László Barabási, *Linked. How Everything Is Connected to Everything and What It Means for Business, Science, and Everyday Life*, New York: Plume, 2003.

9   Not only in terms of how a specific form has come about, but also in terms of how it is going to keep changing.

10   Alexander R. Galloway, *Protocol: How Control Exists after Decentralization*, Cambridge: MIT Press, 2004, in particular Chapter 1.

that they can be sent over the network without loss, they are not the only ones. Also part of the transport layer is the User Datagram Protocol (UDP). UDP is used for establishing low latency and loss-tolerating connections on the internet, like voice over IP or video streaming. In contrast to TCP, which is considered a reliable protocol for host-to-host communication, UDP might lose some of its datagrams according to its best-effort approach, a circumstance that implies an entirely different understanding of what communication is.[11] UDP does not need a 'handshake' to establish a connection before an exchange can happen. It just wants to connect.[12] Consequently, it encapsulates a completely different imaginary than the strict and control-based network of Galloway's imagination. Translated into cultural theory, UDP would evoke the idea of a promiscuous network, corresponding more to George Bataille's general economy than to a rigid reading of Deleuze's postscript on the societies of control.[13]

II.

Why is this of importance? Because networks are not just descriptive, but rather performative. They not only represent the world, they also have real-world effects. Network technologies play a crucial role in the cultural logic of late capitalism because they respond directly to the socio-economic shift that has restructured the global system over the last thirty years.[14] Even though, on the surface, digital capitalism may have solidified into platforms, its underlying structure still follows a network logic.[15] I am not simply talking about the fact that all common platforms (e.g. Amazon, Facebook, Google, Netflix, Spotify) still rely on the material, and so protocological, infrastructure of the internet, but that, in a very literal sense, the network, or rather the analytical diagram based on networks, constitutes the 'motor' of these platforms. Network analytics is far from being dead.[16] It continues to fuel capitalist value production in its digital form by providing the tools to sift through the ever-increasing amount of data and extract from it fast-selling information. In doing so, data models are undergirded by the homophilic assumption that the friend of my friend might also be a suitable friend for me.[17]

11   John Durham Peters's introduction to *Speaking into the Air* for a comprehensive account of the many facets of the term 'communication'. John Durham Peters, *Speaking into the Air*, Chicago: University of Chicago Press, 1999.

12   In fact, it just wants to be received, without necessarily receiving anything back. For this clarification I want to thank Niels ten Oever, who also made me aware of the fact that with QUIC a general-purpose transport layer network protocol, which was initially designed at Google and uses UDP as its basis, has now been implemented as an equivalent to TCP.

13   Compare Galloway, *Protocol*, p. 81. On the idea of a 'promiscuous network', see also Wendy Hui Kyong Chun and Sarah Friedland, 'Habits of Leaking: Of Sluts and Network Cards', *differences* 26.2 (2015): 1-28.

14   Wendy Hui Kyong Chun, 'Networks NOW: Belated too Early', in David M. Berry and Michael Dieter (eds) *Postdigital Aesthetics. Art, Computation and Design*, London: Palgrave Macmillan, 2015, pp. 290-316.

15   Marc Steinberg's recent book for an in-depth analysis of how 'platformization' has transformed capitalism over the past decades. Marc Steinberg, *The Platform Economy*, Minneapolis: University of Minnesota Press, 2019.

16   I agree with Geert Lovink that network science as an academic discipline has seen better days (see his article in this volume). However, network theory is alive and kicking, not least because it found its way into nonacademic fields and economic applications.

17   Wendy Hui Kyong Chun, 'Queerying Homophily', in Clemens Apprich, Wendy Hui Kyong Chun, Florian Cramer, and Hito Steyerl (eds.) *Pattern Discrimination*, Minneapolis/Lüneburg: University of Minnesota

We are constantly being lumped together, in order to predict our buying behavior, our credit, or our desirability score. The network has become such a powerful force today, because it determines how the world sees us and, by the same token, how we see the world. It would therefore be negligent to disregard the still central role that networks play in the constitution of our subjectivity. As linked-up data bundles we have reached a crossroads with regards to our networked future. On the one hand, we are facing a systemic stupidity, which declares everything, even our luggage, to be connected and smart, thereby yielding nothing more than a stale repetition of consumerism.[18] On the other hand, there are socio-technical networks at our fingertips, which enable true innovation by virtue of their transindividual potential. Today it is possible for individuals to be part of different social spheres at the same time. We are thus, potentially, traversed by different networks and open to diverse associations as the precondition for a genuine – because collective – subjectivity.[19]

According to Katherine Hayles this subjectivity is not only characterized by traversing different social networks, but also by the transition from deep to hyper attention.[20] Today's subject is embedded in a digital and networked environment with the effect that (human) cognition gears toward hyper attentiveness. In contrast to deep attention, which is associated with traditional knowledge acquisition and involves single information streams and long focus times, hyper attention is characterized by the ability to quickly scan significant amounts of data and combine them in certain, albeit ephemeral patterns. This generational shift in cognitive styles is supported by the thesis that humans and technology have always co-evolved, in the sense that human beings and technical artifacts are mutually amplified.[21] What is new, according to Hayles, is the fact that with digital media networks and media-rich environments, the speed of such an ontogenetic evolution across generations has increased significantly. Technical systems, according to Hayles and others, affect the physiological wiring of the brain, and altered human cognition in turn stimulates technological development.[22] In this reciprocity, new cognitive assemblages emerge, which differ from networks in the way that they enable contiguity in a 'fleshly sense' and make dynamic interactions between human and nonhuman cognizers tangible.[23] Inspired by neuroscience and cognitive science, the

        Press/meson press, 2019, pp. 59-97.

18   On the notion of 'systemic stupidity', see Bernard Stiegler, *Automatic Society. Volume 1: The Future of Work*, Cambridge: Polity Press, 2016, pp. 24f.

19   Clemens Apprich, *Technotopia, A Media Genealogy of Net Cultures*, London: Rowman & Littlefield International, 2017, pp. 126ff.

20   N. Katherine Hayles, 'Hyper and Deep Attention: The Generational Divide in Cognitive Modes', *Profession* (2007): 187-199.

21   Bernard Stiegler, *Technics and Time, 1: The Fault of Epimetheus*, Palo Alto: Stanford University Press, 1998.

22   Nicholas Carr, *The Shallows: What the Internet Is Doing to Our Brains*, New York: Norton & Company, 2011; N. Katherine Hayles, *How We Think: Digital Media and Contemporary Technogenesis*, Chicago: University of Chicago Press, 2012.

23   N. Katherine Hayles, *Unthought. The Power of the Cognitive Nonconscious*, Chicago: The University of Chicago Press, 2017, p. 118. Hayles asserts that networks, in contrast to assemblages, cannot account for interactions across complex three-dimensional topologies, however this claim has been proven wrong by artificial neural networks, which do operate in n-dimensional spaces.

idea behind Hayles's work is to acknowledge various roles of cognition in human and nonhuman life, thereby granting cognitive agency to technical devices as well.

Like other approaches in new materialism or speculative realism, such as actor-network theory (ANT) or object-oriented ontology (OOO), Hayles objects to an anthropocentric view of the world. Similarly to Jane Bennett, a prominent figure of new materialism, she attributes agential powers to assemblages of human and nonhuman actors, which are able to perform cognitive tasks.[24] Although this line of thinking is highly ambiguous,[25] the redistribution of agency across a network of actants follows the material turn toward what Manuel DeLanda coined as a 'flat ontology'.[26] Within this ontology, assemblages form on the surface of the material world and allow for an ontogenetic understanding of materiality. They are, in this sense, the analogue counterpart to digital networks. While digital networks follow the binary and abstracted logic of inclusion and exclusion,[27] assemblages invoke quantitative and qualitative continua.[28] Beyond a symbolic construction of reality, the assemblage enacts the idea that all things exist equally. Instead of viewing the world through human experience, new materialists assert that there is no privileged ontological status of one thing over another. They ask for new forms of critique that dump the social, that is symbolically constructed, reality of postmodern thinking. Human reasoning, in this reading, is not sufficient to explain complex cognitive processes, such as interpretation, decision, and choice. Access to reality is not only mediated by higher consciousness, but also interpenetrated by technical systems. It is therefore no surprise when Geoffrey Hinton, godfather of so-called connectionism, a branch of AI research that promotes artificial neural networks, takes the same line by claiming that reasoning is the last step in what we call thinking.[29] In accordance with Hayles's cognitive pyramid, reasoning as part of conscious modes of awareness is built on top of nonconscious cognition, which is built on material processes.[30]

III.

My aim in this essay is not to pit networks against assemblages, which would be futile as they have more in common than not, but rather to show why the concept of assemblages is put

---

24   Hayles, *Unthought*, p. 175.
25   Graham Harman's blog introduction to object-oriented philosophy and how it differs from speculative realism. Graham Harman, 'brief SR/OOO tutorial', *Object-Oriented Philosophy,* 23 July 2010, https://doctorzamalek2.wordpress.com/2010/07/23/brief-srooo-tutorial.
26   Manuel DeLanda, *Intensive Science and Virtual Philosophy*, London: Continuum, 2002, pp. 46f.
27   Manuel Castells, 'Informationalism, Networks, and the Network Society: A Theoretical Blueprint', in Manuel Castells et al. (eds) *The Network Society. A Cross-Cultural Perspective*, Northampton: Edward Elgar Publishing, 2004, pp. 36-45. Following this logic, the network only exists if its nodes and the links between these nodes are activated. If a node is not useful to the network it is switched off.
28   Galloway even speaks of a new 'analogicity' in contemporary thinking, with a turn toward affect, aesthetics, empiricism, pragmatism, and new materialism. See his talk 'The Concept of the Digital', the Institute of the Humanities and Global Cultures, University of Virginia, 18 March 2019, https://www.youtube.com/watch?v=eq4CDLNAvXU.
29   Geoffrey Hinton, 'Turing Award Lecture. The Deep Learning Revolution', Federated Computing Research Conference, 2018, https://www.youtube.com/watch?v=VsnQf7exv5I.
30   Hayles, *Unthought*, pp. 39f.

forward as an alternative to networks in current debates about digital cultures. Although I am well aware that the heterogenous approaches in new materialist thinking cannot be lumped together, I am wondering – as does Galloway – why contemporary theoretical models of flat ontology resemble, in so many aspects, the latest drive toward technocapitalism.[31] In particular speculative realism (see Quentin Meillassoux) and object-oriented ontology (see Graham Harman), both of which have resisted alignment with the broader project of new materialism, can be seen to express the conditions of a fully-automated capitalist society, comprised of human and notably nonhuman actors. These philosophies defy any form of symbolic abstraction thereby turning against reason itself. In philosophical realism nothing lies outside the real and, as a consequence, ontology comes before epistemology. As such, proponents of a flat ontology are not interested in the possibility of critically reflecting the world. Epistemic access to the world is simply another relation on a flat ontological plane.[32] Why is this of concern? Because the rejection of epistemology is consistent with the claim that all theory has ended.[33] Deeply rooted in what was once called Californian Ideology,[34] this claim mirrors the technocapitalist promises of the 90s. In an odd twist in the history of the present, we are witnessing the revival of a hackneyed idea: a self-referential economic system, inspired by biology and operating on autopoiesis.[35] The idea of ontogenetic evolution thus plays right into an ideology that, by default, conceals (human) labor in order to uphold the fetish of self-generating value production. What is new in digital technocapitalism is the fact that complex and elaborated algorithms push toward the transformation of the mode of production by fine-tuning the value extraction process.

There is clearly a problem here in terms of possibilities for critique. While algorithmic subsumption has become real, the idea of criticizing, let alone changing, this reality is dismissed by contemporary philosophy. If everything is as important as anything else, then nothing really matters and no political decision must be made.[36] Granted, things are a little more complicated than that. Given today's complex and entangled world, the advantages of a productive attentiveness to material processes or the destabilization of the Western subject with its 'enlightened' rationalism are undeniable. However the negative conception of knowledge, based on the thesis that the world either recedes (Harman) or resists (Hayles) human rationality, leaves us without any possibility to – at least intellectually – engage with it.

31   Alexander R. Galloway, 'The Poverty of Philosophy: Realism and Post-Fordism', *Critical Inquiry* 39.2
      (Winter 2013): 347-366.
32   For a critical account of flat ontology see Ray Brassier, 'Deleveling: Against "Flat Ontologies"' in Channa
      van Dijk et al. (eds) *Under Influence – Philosophical Festival Drift*, Amsterdam: Omnia, 2015, pp. 64-80.
33   Chris Anderson, 'The End of Theory: Will the Data Deluge Make the Scientific Method Obsolete?', *Wired
      Magazine*, 23 June 2008, https://www.wired.com/2008/06/pb-theory.
34   Richard Barbrook and Andy Cameron, 'The Californian Ideology', in Josephine Berry Slater and Pauline
      van Mourik Broekman (eds) *Proud to Be Flesh: A Mute Magazine Anthology of Cultural Politics After the
      Net*, London: Mute Publishing with Autonomedia, 2009, pp. 27-34.
35   Kevin Kelly, *Out of Control. The New Biology of Machines, Social Systems, and the Economic World*, New
      York: Basic Books, 1994.
36   As Nina Power put it: 'proliferating ontologies is simply not the point – [...] what use is it if it simply
      becomes a race to the bottom to prove that every entity is as meaningless as every other (besides,
      the Atomists did it better).' Nina Power, 'The Dialectics of Nature', cited in Galloway, 'The Poverty of
      Philosophy'.

If one cannot know what an object is in itself, all that is left to know is when one's conception of this object fails to work.[37] But how does one know when it fails if there is no knowledge of what an object, and so one's relation to this object, really is? How can we discriminate between nonconscious processes and discrete real objects? If the nonconscious represents a large part of human cognition and is – in contrast to unconscious mental processes – inaccessible to analysis, then any attempt to understand the world around us must fail. Yet, at the same time, there are good arguments for the idea that reality is not simply flattened but stratified – or maybe even networked.[38] As I initially noted, the idea of the network is not so much geared toward what something *is*, but rather how it *works*. In this respect, the epistemological question is still of relevance. Especially so, as algorithms, that is knowable objects that can be reverse engineered,[39] structure our perception of the world. Against a flat ontology, I want to argue for an epistemology that takes human as well as other experiences into account when it comes to an increasingly data-driven reality. Here we can see a return of the network on a micro-level: whereas the 90s was all about network politics on a macro-level,[40] recently the network has creeped into every fiber of the so-called digital service industry (Apple, Amazon, Google, Facebook, Microsoft). Working on the premise of clustering and segmentation, these platforms primarily involve the monetization of user activity based on network parameters.[41]

One might fairly object that I haven't offered an account of the further potential of networks so far. The repetitive, yet differentiating, faculty becomes clear when we think again of the 'identity politics' of digital networks. The prevailing assumption that birds of a feather flock together,[42] has without doubt turned the emancipatory idea of social media into one of poorly gated networks of homophily.[43] Yet these new modes of identification are not merely a repetition of the same; they enable a constant proliferation. With each repetition, the network actualizes a slightly different identity, a fact that can be witnessed in the work of data analytics companies. As John Cheney-Lippold has shown, the networked infrastructure of the internet, and the subsequent ability to track user behavior, has led to a 'new algorithmic identity', based on statistical inference to determine one's age, class, gender, and race.[44] The interesting

37   Holger Pötzsch, 'Posthumanism, Technogenesis, and Digital Technologies: A Conversation with N. Katherine Hayles', *The Fibreculture Journal* 23 (2014), http://twentythree.fibreculturejournal.org/fcj-172-posthumanism-technogenesis-and-digital-technologies-a-conversation-with-katherine-n-hayles.
38   Ray Brassier, 'Deleveling', p. 79.
39   At least this is the assumption of critical software or code studies. See Matthew Fuller, *Behind the Blip. Essays on the Culture of Software*, New York: Autonomedia, 2003.
40   Albert Arnold Gore, 'Remarks on the National Information Infrastructure at the National Press Club', 21 December 1993, http://www.ibiblio.org/nii/goremarks; Martin Bangemann et al., 'Bangemann Report: Europe and the Global Information Society' (1994), http://cordis.europa.eu/news/rcn/2730_en.html; International Telecommunications Unit, 'Declaration of Principles. Building the Information Society: a global challenge in the new Millennium', 12 December 2003, https://www.itu.int/net/wsis/docs/geneva/official/dop.html.
41   The actual nuts and bolts of data analysis entails finding 'similarities' between distinct network nodes (or, users).
42   Miller McPherson, Lynn Smith-Lovin, and James M. Cook, 'Birds of a Feather: Homophily in Social Networks', *Annual Review of Sociology* 27 (2001): 415-444.
43   Chun, 'Queerying Homophily'.
44   John Cheney-Lippold, 'A New Algorithmic Identity: Soft Biopolitics and the Modulation of Control', *Theory Culture* & *Society* 28.6 (2011): 164-181.

aspect of Cheney-Lippold's argument is that these 'hard categories' are not found from one crop of data, but are constantly (re)actualized. Each time a user moves from one web page to another, the identity categories are updated.[45] Hence a user's ascribed gender can and may change as new data about them is gathered. The algorithms, initially built to enable marketers to target users with advertising, content, and services, allow for a fluid formation of identity, which transmutes with each cycle.[46] What is more, the fluidity of this algorithmic identity also affects its categorization, so that from the algorithm's point of view, it is totally fine if the user is 58 percent male, 32 percent female, and 10 percent 'other'. However, at some point a decision has to be made whether the user belongs in this or that category, because the data eventually serves a real-world purpose (marketing). The problem here then is not so much that algorithms help make sense of an ever-increasing data stream, but that capitalist logic necessitates a retrograde identity politics. The identity is not found in the subject as such, rather the subject's identity is constructed on the basis of very specific network analytics, which mimics the underlying assumptions of a (racist, sexist, and otherwise discriminating) society. Yet such technology could be put to work differently, for different purposes and ends. Again, we find ourselves at a crossroads. One sign points to a 'reticular pessimism', where a networked mode of control predetermines every possible outcome.[47] Another sign points to a new algorithmic reality, which, if its contingency is embraced, might lead to a new politics of possibility.[48] In this sense, the story of the network truly is never-ending.

---

45   In the same manner an artificial neural network, when applied to the 'real' world, is never effectively
      trained off, because with each interaction (e.g. a user-request via a virtual assistant) the whole network
      – respectively its weights – re-adjusts. This also hints to the 'social' component of these systems, whose
      categories are actualized on the basis of not only one, but multiple users.
46   A good example of the fluidity of a data-encoded identity is *Probably Chelsea*, an artwork by
      Heather Dewey-Hagborg: thirty variations of possible portraits of Chelsea Manning that have been
      algorithmically generated by an analysis of her DNA. The artwork 'shows just how many ways your DNA
      can be interpreted as data, and how subjective the act of reading DNA really is. [...] It is a refutation
      of outmoded notions of biologically inscribed identity and a testament to the commonality of all, a
      molecular solidarity that is clearly present even at the cellular level.' Heather Dewey-Hagborg, 'Probably
      Chelsea Manning', https://deweyhagborg.com/projects/probably-chelsea.
47   Alexander R. Galloway, 'Network Pessimism', *Culture and Communication*, 11 November 2014, http://
      cultureandcommunication.org/galloway/network-pessimism.
48   Louise Amore, *The Politics of Possibility. Risk and Security Beyond Probability*, Durham: Duke University
      Press, 2013.

NETWORKS AND LIFE-WORLDS: ENDS AND ENDINGS

DAPHNE DRAGONA

NETWORKS AND LIFE-WORLDS:
ENDS AND ENDINGS

DAPHNE DRAGONA

It might, at first, seem arbitrary to relate the ends of networks to the so-called 'end/s of the world'. The 'ends' of a network are its nodes: the points connected through, and bounded by, its lines, forming topologies that usually have the potential to be expanded by the addition of more ends, or nodes, to the system. Originating in graph theory, networks are often understood as the 'abstract formulation' of elements that can have social, informational, technological, or biological manifestations.[1] References to 'the end of the world' might be metaphorical or literal, depending on era, culture, and/or context. As Gabrys explains,[2] worlds – plural – have always been ending, due to settler colonialism, environmental racism, and ecological exhaustion. Nowadays, the expression 'world endings' is mostly used as 'the default script'[3] of the climate crisis in order to discuss its '(anthropic) causes and (catastrophic) consequences';[4] it implies forms of elimination, power, and dis/possession. Within this context, as one may understand from Gabrys's work, the role of networks is crucial, and that is because it is the networked, sensing infrastructures that provide environmental data regarding the possible ends of living worlds. However, networks, at their conceptual inception, were not necessarily meant to be associated with endings.

As Fritjof Capra explained, two decades ago, in his book *Web of Life*,[5] network architectures assist us in understanding what holds the living world together. 'Whenever we see life, we see networks',[6] he argues. Capra uses the eponymous term 'web of life' to refer to 'networks within networks', 'systems nesting within other systems.'[7] A 'node', in this case, is an organism which itself constitutes a living network, while having its place in a larger, complex architecture that is nonhierarchical and always in a state of 'open balance'. Such living networks, for Capra, greatly differ from other technological or social networks in having the capacity to constantly evolve, grow, and self-regulate: these are networks that are able to constantly 'make themselves'.[8] Capra was convinced that we could learn a lot about the principles of

---

1   Alexander R. Galloway and Eugene Thacker, *The Exploit: A Theory of Networks*, Minneapolis: University of Minnesota Press, 2007, p. 34.
2   Jennifer Gabrys, 'Ocean Sensing and Navigating the End of this World', *e-flux* 101 (2019), https://www.e-flux.com/journal/101/272633/ocean-sensing-and-navigating-the-end-of-this-world/.
3   Gabrys, 'Ocean Sensing'.
4   Deborah Danowski and Eduardo Viveiros de Castro, *The Ends of the World*, transl. Rodrigo Nunes, Cambridge/Malden: Polity Press, 2017, p. 1.
5   Fritjof Capra, *The Web of Life*, New York: Anchor Books, 1996.
6   Fritjof Capra, 'The Web of Life', 3rd annual Schrödinger Lecture, Trinity College Dublin, Ireland, 9 September 1997, https://pdfs.semanticscholar.org/bfb6/c6a3bdfb66ad7016b6a43e18cc213bb0556b.pdf.
7   Capra, *The Web of Life*, p. 5.
8   Here Capra refers to the biologists Humberto Maturana and FranciscoVarela, who famously spoke of the process of autopoiesis. Capra, 'The Web of Life'.

ecology and the 'language of nature' from studying what he saw as the self-regulation of the living world and the networks that comprise it. His interest lay in mapping and understanding these networks, their patterns, interdependences and interrelationships. In keeping with systems thinking and cybernetics, Capra turned to networks, as a means to examine and comprehend the Earth's ecosystems, their architectures and metabolisms.

Rereading Capra's work nowadays invites us to reflect upon the application of the concept of networks to the Earth's life-worlds, with the latter understood as ecosystems:[9] the possibility to pass from the parts to the whole manifests the human desire of the human for a holistic vision of the living world.[10] From the 60s on, the Earth came to be understood as a network of networks, the planet as a living body – an object that could be both studied and controlled. Already with the first planetary infrastructures – the satellite systems – as Gabrys reminds us quoting McLuhan, the Earth became programmable, opening the way for 'new configurations [...] across technologies, people, practices and nonhuman entities.'[11] Ever since that time, networked systems have been used to capture information and to render the Earth's life-worlds not only legible but also sensible and available for attempts at their management and optimization. Thanks to satellites, drones, sensors and robotic entities, acting as nodes of highly complex systems, it has become possible to monitor environmental conditions – the quality of the air, the soil, the waters of the oceans – and, increasingly, to navigate,[12] as new entanglements of machinic and more-than-human entities come into existence.

This approach to the Earth as a 'pilotable machine' is defined by Frédéric Neyrat as 'geo-constructivism'.[13] At the heart of it, he explains, lies the fundamental fantasy that 'the Earth and everything contained on it, the ecosystems and the organisms, humans and non-humans can and must be reconstructed and entirely remade.'[14] Programming is no longer enough: now the urge is to 'repair, to reprogram, to reconstruct' the planet,[15] making use of science and technology to measure climate change, forecast natural disasters and other phenomena. This points to current discussions on 'terraforming'. Albeit this term is mostly used to refer to how *other* planets could be modified to become habitable for humans, it is also a belief held by many that the Earth itself must undergo such processes in order to remain viable for its own life-forms.[16] Thus, in Neyrat's terms, a 'strange topology' unfolds, with the geo-constructivists speculatively regarding themselves as 'residing off-planet', detached from Earth's ecosystems, so that Earth can be reformatted as an object.[17]

---

9   The term was first coined by the British ecologist Arthur Tansley in 1936, and was further developed by
     G. Evelyn Hutchinson, and, later, Howard T. Odum and Eugene P. Odum.
10   Capra, *The Web of Life*, pp. 18-35.
11   This is a reference to the first Earth satellite, Sputnik. Jennifer Gabrys, *Program Earth: Environmental
     Sensing Technology and the Making of a Computational Planet*, Minneapolis: University Minnesota Press,
     2015, p. 4.
12   Gabrys, 'Ocean Sensing and Navigating the End of this World'.
13   Frédéric Neyrat, *The Unconstructable Earth: An Ecology of Separation*, trans. Drew S. Burk, New York:
     Fordham University Press, 2018, p. 1.
14   Neyrat, *The Unconstructable Earth*, p. 2.
15   Neyrat, *The Unconstructable Earth*, pp. 2f.
16   Benjamin Bratton, *The Terraforming*, Moscow: Strelka Press, 2019.
17   Neyrat, *The Unconstructable Earth*, p. 5.

Networks, therefore, as currently related to the understanding, attempted management, and possible remaking of the living world, are thus simultaneously associated with its possible endings and, potentially, its new, human-made beginnings. Within this framework, questions about the actors and the interests involved must come to the fore. In his 2015 book *Capitalism and the Web of Life*, Jason W. Moore highlights the ways in which capitalism has organized what is called now 'nature', and opened up the way for forms of exploitation within and between cultures, populations, lands, and territories.[18] Should the claim for a 'reparation ecology' arise, then, as Holly Jean Buck reminds us, pointing to Moore's work with Raj Patel, and the work of Donna Haraway, several other 're-s' must also be taken into consideration – from recognition to redistribution, and from reimagination to recreation or recomposition,[19] all of which would involve very different processes than the attempted remaking, reprogramming and restoration of the climate and the planet which prominent contemporary scientific and technological approaches indicate.

How, then, might networks be reconsidered within the context of the planet's restoration? Could the web of life be understood, instead – in terms of 'nature as us, inside us, around us'[20] – as an open process of 'life-making', with 'no basic units, only webs within webs of relations: "worlds within worlds"'?[21] Are there networks that could 'suggest strategies for sensing, mapping, navigating and inventing worlds otherwise'?[22] Could artistic practices assist in reimagining the role of networks? In addressing these questions, I will now introduce and examine the critical approaches and methodologies of four artistic projects, which, in my opinion, offer grounds for a discussion of different kinds of planetary infrastructures and/or sensory networks, in specific cultural, geographical, and ecological contexts, and which exemplify the ways in which specific technologies influence the understanding and survival of life-worlds.

18   As Moore notes, the rise of capitalism gave us the idea not only that society was relatively independent of the web of life, but also that most women, indigenous peoples, slaves, colonized people were not fully human and thus not full members of society. Jason W. Moore, *Capitalism in the Web of Life: Ecology and the Accumulation of Capital*. London/New York: Verso, 2015.
19   Holly Jean Buck, *After Geoengineering: Climate Tragedy, Repair and Restoration*, London/New York: Verso, 2019, p. 245.
20   Moore, *Capitalism in the Web of Life*, p. 3.
21   Moore, *Capitalism in the Web of Life*, pp. 7f.
22   Gabrys, 'Ocean Sensing and Navigating the End of this World'.

Geocinema

Asia Bazdyrieva, Alexey Orlov, and Solveig Suess initiated the *Geocinema* project in order to examine how planetary scale sensory networks, such as satellites, surveillance cameras, geosensors, and cell phones, formulate the way that we see the world and its environmental changes.[23] As in Benjamin Bratton's words, there is a way in which the climate crisis is 'a figural truth that is composited together from thousands of different kinds of sensing, each drawing a partial image.'[24] It is only by the bringing-together of these infrastructures of different scales and temporalities, and the stitching-together of the raw data, that a representation of the world and its changing climate can be produced. *Geocinema* is the name given by this project's creators to what they describe as a 'vastly distributed cinematic apparatus' which can be used to remind us that there is not one Earth, but many, 'always composite [...] stitched together into a montage of the world'[25] – *Geocinema* comprises multiple angles, edits, and viewings.

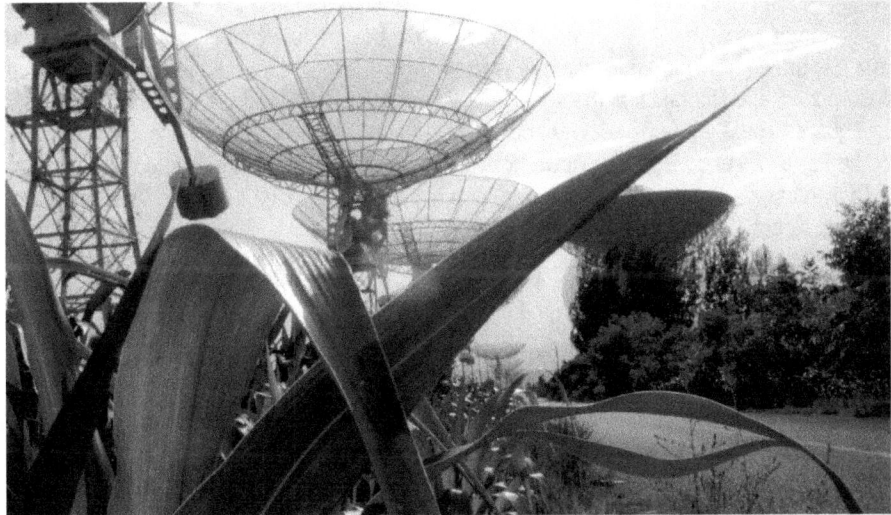

Fig. 1: Geocinema, Framing Territories, 2019 (film still).

For the production of the work the team conducted lengthy field trips and in-depth research, exploring the planetary network of Earth-observatories, with a focus on certain crucial nodes in Asia. One of these is DBAR (Digital Belt and Road) in China – the Big Earth Data counterpart to

23   The *Geocinema* project was developed as part of The New Normal, a speculative urbanism programme at the Strelka Institute of Media, Architecture and Design, Moscow. A section of the project, *Geocinema: Framing Territories* was commissioned as part of The New Networked Normal (NNN), a 2019 partnership and program co-funded by the EU. The New Networked Normal, https://geocinema. network/.

24   'Geocinema project presentation', The New Normal 2018 Final Project Review, Strelka Institute Moscow, June 2018, https://www.youtube.com/watch?v=UXIZdifwolE.

25   'Geocinema project presentation', The New Normal 2018 Final Project Review.

the Belt and Road Initiative[26] – which aims to operate 'as a digital nervous system of the globe, providing information about the events happening on (or close to) the Earth's surface',[27] while engaging in a continuous rendering process.[28] The artists studied how weather-forecasting is made possible, and how it is intertwined with political and economic agendas, manifesting power asymmetries between territories. As part of their research they also examined the impact on the Earth's body of the manufacture and construction of infrastructures that are dependent on the extraction of rare-earth materials. Both the locations of the network's nodes – in this case, Earth-observatories – and the sites of extractivism, relate to the making of pasts, presents and futures.

Geocinema also comments on the 'geopolitics of resolution', a new form of governance that operates through imaging – and thus allowing us to see – the world as we think we know it.[29] The project affirms the idea that, as T. J. Demos argues, the colonization of nature and the colonization of its representation go hand in hand, making use of anthropocenic imagery to reinforce the position that once 'we' have mastered the imaging of nature, 'we' have also mastered nature itself.[30] The final work included in the project is a documentary based on imagery drawn from planetary scale sensory networks. Such 'readymade material' is reused, repurposed, and stitched together[31] with interviews by the artists with data scientists, activists, and guards from featured sites. With the aim of queering common narratives about the image of the Earth and encourage the viewer to embrace multiple new world-perspectives, the film is to a great extent narrated by a human, or more-than-human, geo-narrator who takes the viewer to locations across the planet.

Asunder

In their project *Asunder,* Tega Brain, Julian Oliver, and Bengt Sjölén address the representation and engineering of the Earth via an examination of the role of machine learning. Vast amounts of the big data now being captured by environmental media are processed by artificial neural networks rather than human brains. *Asunder* takes as its starting point the potential of Generative Adversarial Networks (GANs) to create images from datasets and satellite imagery.[32] In relation to the ongoing discourse about the potential of AI to monitor and manage natural resources, this project's creators ask: What challenges arise in relation to the use of

---

26 DBAR is part of the Belt and Road Initiative (BRI). BRI is a long-term policy and investment program aimed at infrastructural and economic development along the route of the historic Silk Road, from Beijing to Bangkok and across vast areas of Central Asia and into Europe.

27 Asia Bazdyrieva and Solveig Suess, 'Future Cinema' (working title), unpublished draft for publication in an upcoming issue of the *e-flux Architecture* journal.

28 This vision originates with Clinton's vice-president Al Gore, who introduced it as another way of understanding the world based on advanced technologies such as geo-information systems, global positioning systems, communication networks, sensor webs, etc.

29 Geocinema, 'Geocinema in conversation with Jussi Parikka', 2018, https://soundcloud.com/user-406692767/geocinema-in-conversation-with-jussi-parikka.

30 T. J. Demos, *Against the Anthropocene: Visual Culture and Environment Today,* Berlin/New York: Sternberg Press, 2017, p. 28.

31 Stephanie Hessler, *Prospecting Ocean,* Cambridge, MA: The MIT Press, 2019.

32 Asunder, https://asunder.earth/.

machine decision-making when it comes to optimizing Earth's landscapes and ecosystems? Whose interests are served by its use in this context, and what would happen if *human* needs were not in the foreground? Reflecting upon processes of inclusion and exclusion that are now inherent to the design and programming of various systems, Tega Brain talks about the need for a form of 'eccentric engineering' whereby existing technologies could be repurposed to include a wider diversity of agendas and perspectives, and to keep in mind life-forms other than the human. This is a call for a rethinking of the 'biases and scopes' of what 'success and failure' are considered to be, when it comes to technologies of geoengineering.[33]

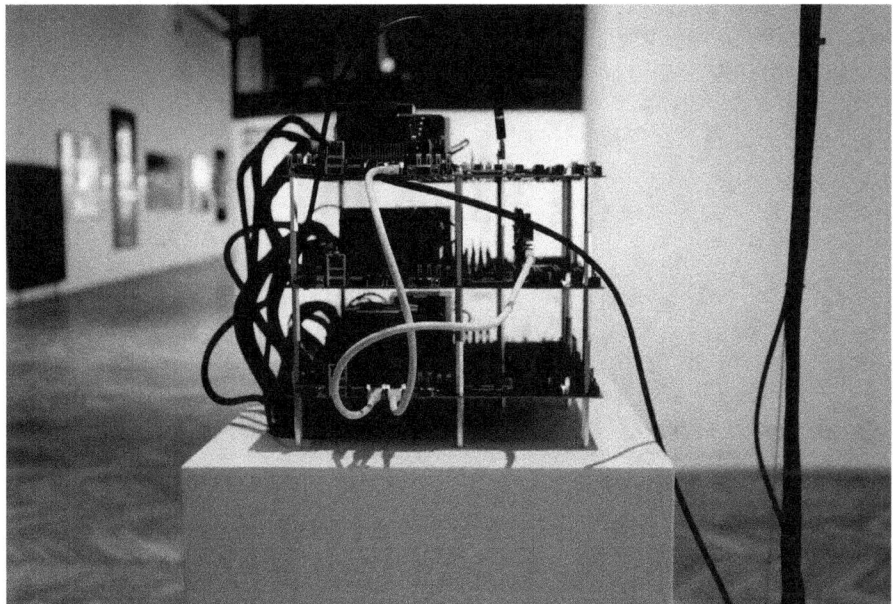

Fig. 2: Tega Brain, Julian Oliver, Bengt Sjölén, Asunder, 2019 (installation view).

Asunder is a project that, while speculative in character, is based on real data drawn from specific regions, arising from a climate modeling system[34] that is able not only to make forecasts but also to propose specific improvements and modifications. The installation presents original satellite images of regions, provides specific details about environmental conditions there, and presents the landscape modifications proposed by the system. As the artists comment about the work, unexpected scenarios and design strategies appear within the installation: cities are relocated, nations are combined and coastlines are straightened.[35] Thus, the project playfully and provocatively discusses and calls into question approaches to geoengineering, imagining what restoration and/or rewilding could mean, for example; speculating on what worlds might end, and what worlds might proliferate, depending on how

---

33 Tega Brain, *Eccentric Engineering blog*, http://blog.eccentric.engineering/about/.
34 The work runs on the CESM model. See University Corporation for Atmospheric Research, 'Community Earth System Model', http://www.cesm.ucar.edu/.
35 Asunder, https://asunder.earth/.

the agendas in play are 'weighted'. In a way, as Buck notes, 'the hard thing isn't beginning the project, but ending it: ensuring that what comes *after geoengineering* is livable.'[36] This is of particular relevance to the present moment, at which more emphasis is currently placed on research and far less on deployment.[37] That is to say, that the ends and endings are not quite in view.

Deep Steward

Machine Wilderness, an art and science initiative connected to the *FoAM* network[38] and initiated by Theun Karelse speaks of 'technologies of loneliness'[39] that 'violate natural processes, disturb habitats and crush biodiversity'.[40] They ask why design technologies are human-centered in the first place, not taking in mind the complexity, biodiversity and different forms of energy of the living environment.

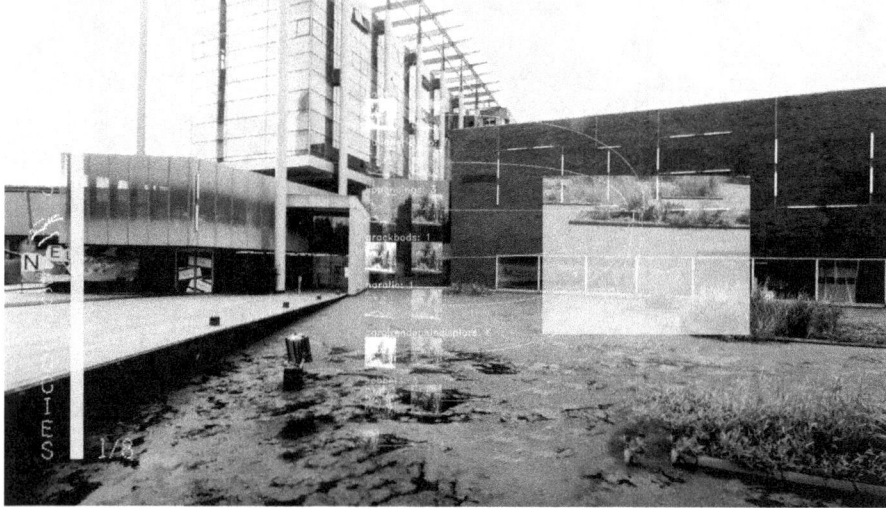

Fig. 3: Klaas Kuitenbrouwer, Theun Karelse, DeepSteward as part of Zoop at Nieuwe Instituut, 2019 (video still).

Machine Wilderness, as the name implies, aims to bring wilderness again to the center of attention, a notion that might be thought as incompatible with technology constituting a 'political free zone where we are able to hide',[41] or possibly something that in a way 'no longer

---

36   Buck, *After Geoengineering,* pp. 26f.
37   Buck, *After Geoengineering,* p. 43.
38   FoAM, https://fo.am/about/.
39   Paraphrastic reference to what Edward O. Wilson terms the 'age of loneliness'. Edward O. Wilson, *Half-Earth: Our Planet's Fight for Life,* New York: Liveright Publishing Corporation, 2016, pp. 71, 73.
40   Machine Wilderness, http://machinewilderness.net/.
41   transmediale, 'Becoming Earth: Engineering Symbiotic Futures', transmediale 2017, https://www.youtube.com/watch?v=RvEZB3tmybs&t=1831s.

exists' and therefore is tried to be preserved in natural parks or similar.[42] A call for wilderness manifests a return of nature, and the potential to re-inhabit the world in a new way.[43] However, the question remains as to which processes can make this possible.

Karelse argues for a form of 'machine wilderness' based on environmental agents; that is, on a form of machine learning that is addressed to, and taught by, the living world – by animals and plants. He draws connections between robotic and biological organisms, and the forms of agency that they have. Karelse and his colleagues work to develop methodologies and projects that are aimed at being of help to living organisms on the one hand, and at improving environmental literacy on the other, helping humans to become aware of the ecosystems to which they belong, and to become conscious participants in them. Their work is conducted via workshops, talks and field trips in different regions, building prototypes of wilderness machines and testing them in specific local situations.

In their explorations of how new forms of more-than-human-oriented environmental AI could inhabit the planet, they embrace 'practices of environmental solidarity, intimacy, affinity, allegiance, reverence, commitment and kinship'.[44] They take the position that it is possible to realize a synthetic 'world view' which acknowledges environmental complexity, once living worlds are given their own voice. This is the specific aim of *DeepSteward* – the project of Ian Ingram and Theun Karelse – which is 'an unsupervised field agent', 'built by humans but left to interpret local trees, local plants, local animals, local geographical features as it sees fit',[45] as well as the project *Zoöp*,[46] a collaboration between Klaas Kuitenbrouwer, Theun Karelse with support by Bas van Koolwijk, whose name is derived from the words 'zoe', the Greek word for life, and 'cooperation'. Here, they speculate about how human, more-than-human and machine entities might possibly all come together on equal terms, in a new entanglement, or assemblage, of wilderness. The project is presented within a floating globe, into which people are invited to insert their head, so as to enter and experience a world of living organisms while it is being captured by infrastructures of different scales and processed by machine intelligence.

Permaculture Network

The potential of networks to empower wilderness is what drove Gary Zhexi Zhang and Agnes Cameron to develop the *Permaculture Network* project.[47] While they were the artists-in-residence of the pedagogical organization Sakiya, based in the village of Ein Qinyya in Palestine, the artists wanted to explore how a mesh network – a local communication system – could grow along with the landscape itself, while respecting and supporting its needs.

42   Wilson, *Half-Earth*, pp. 71, 73.
43   Neyrat, *The Unconstructable Earth*, p. 162.
44   Random Forests, http://randomforest.nl/.
45   Theun Karelse and Ian Ingram, 'Deep Steward', *FoAM blog*, 17 April 2019, https://fo.am/blog/2019/04/17/deep-steward/.
46   'Ecologies', *Neuhaus blog*, https://neuhaus.hetnieuweinstituut.nl/en/premises/zoop-research-facility.
47   The work was commissioned as part of the 'Rigged Systems' Solitude and ZKM Web Residencies, https://schloss-post.com/permaculture-network/.

Interestingly, the area in question has self-rewilded, an ideal situation in terms of ecological conservation and permaculture, however this is because it is part of Area C of the West Bank, where Palestinians are not allowed to build.[48]

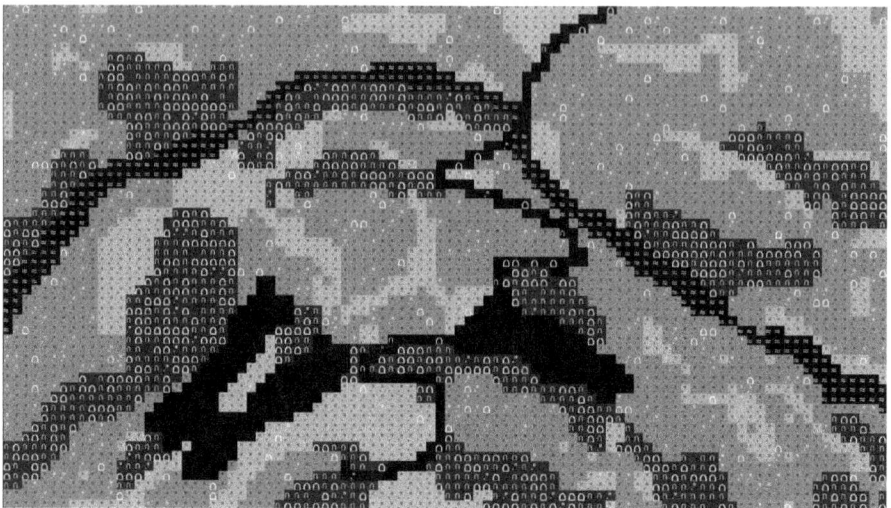

Fig. 4: Gary Zhexi Zhang and Agnes Cameron, Permaculture Network, 2019 (screenshot).

Social and network infrastructures, technological and living systems, political and cultural asymmetries are all featured in this project, in relation to a specific location and its role/s in the emergence of different networks of awareness and resistance. As the artists specifically note, 'there is a direct correlation between [the] measurement of the land and its qualities and its subsequent requisitioning from Palestinian hands, whether as a natural reserve, an archaeological site or an industrial farm, on the pretext of conservation and resource management.'[49]

Ecological, geological, and topographical features also come together in the project's eponymous networked-sensors infrastructure, and its web interface.[50] In the former, local sensors are literally planted on site, and supported by external feeds that provide satellite weather data. As for the latter, the web interface operates as a live simulation, or speculative fiction, of interactions in the living environment, wherein different wild and cultivated species are introduced, along with their supposed personalities and characteristics; imagined dialogues between plants, animals, soil, water, the human and the more-than-human world appear to reveal the dynamics of the soil and the land. The attention paid here to the land and the soil can be read as an artistic interpretation of María Puig de la Bellacasa's writings.[51] The

48   'Flora, Fauna and Folk Tales – A Permaculture Network. Interview with Gary Zhexi Zhang & Agnes
     Cameron', *Schloss Post,* 5 September 2019, https://schloss-post.com/flora-fauna-and-folk-tales/.
49   'Flora, Fauna and Folk Tales'.
50   Schloss Post, http://root.schloss-post.com/.
51   María Puig de la Bellacasa, 'Encountering Bioinfrastructure: Ecological Struggles and the Sciences of
     Soil', *Social Epistemology: A Journal of Knowledge, Culture and Policy* 28.1 (2014): 26-40.

soil, she explains, is not just a container of worlds but a 'world in itself', which is not residual: not fixed, but alive, thanks to all the organisms that inhabit it and offer their invisible labor. The soil is a 'living bioinfrastructure', and therefore perfectly exemplifies the 'web of life', along with the related endangerments. Simulating it and animating it sheds vivid light on its actors and their innumerable valuable movements and interactions.

Having surveyed these four art projects that attempt to reimagine the networked systems that capture changes occurring on the body of planet, affecting its landscapes and ecosystems, what conclusions may be drawn, on the basis of these examples?

The projects here presented address the imbalances of power and agency that characterize environmental media, networks, and infrastructures, whether between territories or between the human and the more-than-human worlds. The projects discuss satellites, artificial neural networks, robotic prototypes and sensory networks in relation to the problematics of monitoring the living world, as well as their potential for being repurposed to build both new forms of awareness and/or actual alternatives.

The creators of all four projects seem to agree that the first step in any strategy of repair must be a much-needed change of perspective. The urge for a more-than-human point of view is expressed in different ways in all of the projects. However speculative these presentations might appear – a story told through a film, a selection of artificially generated images, an environmental AI prototype, a simulation of interactions – each project has taken as their starting point existing resources, real data sets, experiential knowledge. And in all of these projects, the human is decentered; human political and economic interests either have no place at all, or are called into question. This can be understood as a form of 'doing speculatively',[52] a necessary practice if we are to imagine anew systemic transformations: as Jussi Parikka notes, models and simulations are 'technologies of knowing' that help us to articulate the reality of abstractions.[53]

Seeing and understanding the world from multiple points of view speaks to the need for a new form of literacy that is both environmental and infrastructural. Against the vaunted promise of proposed human-centered interventions on a grand scale, such as climate-engineering, these projects argue for systems and networks of knowledge that can inform us as to how ecosystems operate, how technologies can and do intervene, and which life-worlds are – or are not – well-supported by such interventions. Could it be that the potential for the emergence of what (after Haraway) could be described as 'kin-making technologies' might lie here, among these different approaches to the projected reprogramming or remaking of the planet? Any such technologies must acknowledge the preexisting forms of affinity found within the living world, respect the underlying network or web of life and aim to support it,

52 Sophie Toupin and Spideralex, 'Introduction: Radical Feminist Storytelling and Speculative Fiction: Creating new worlds by re-imagining hacking', *Ada: A Journal of Gender New Media & Technology* 13 (2018), https://adanewmedia.org/2018/05/issue13-toupin-spideralex/.

53 Jussi Parikka, 'Abstractions – and How to be Here and There at the Same Time', *FNG Research* 3.3 (May 2019), https://research.fng.fi/2019/05/24/abstractions-and-how-to-be-here-and-there-at-the-same-time/.

prioritizing the viability of existing habitats. The creation of kin-making technologies involves acts of recuperation as well as acts of effecting sympoiesis between machinic and more-than-human environments:[54] the creator comes in to design and/or repurpose systems to see beyond the interests and needs of the human.

As Déborah Danowski argues, 'when the end of the world is reached, an entire new world, even if so desired, is impossible.'[55] Reprogramming or remaking the world is not achievable either, and this is most likely a disorientating direction for societies to face in, away from their real responsibilities for effecting change.[56] What is still possible, though, is to invent 'new ways of living with what we have, in the ruins of the present world.'[57] It is, principally, relationships that need to be repaired, not just landscapes, the atmosphere, the climate.[58] Returning to the network as a model for understanding the world, from this relational perspective, it is not just the nodes, or ends, that need to be taken care of; it is the 'lines' as well — the connections that hopefully might prevent the acceleration of the world's human-made endings.

54   Donna Haraway, *Staying with the Trouble: Making Kin in the Chthulucene*, Durham: Duke University Press, 2016.
55   Déborah Danowski and Krystian Woznicki, 'Welcoming the Ends of the World: an interview with philosopher Déborah Danowski about the problem that "there are too few people with too much world, and too many people with way too little"', *Mediapart blog,* 8 April 2019, https://blogs.mediapart.fr/krystian-woznicki/blog/080419/welcoming-ends-world.
56   Neyrat, *The Unconstructable Earth*, p. 33.
57   Danowski and Woznicki, 'Welcoming the Ends of the World'.
58   Buck, *After Geoengineering*, p. 44.

THERE ARE WORDS AND WORLDS THAT ARE TRUTHFUL AND TRUE

Luiza Prado de O. Martins

THERE ARE WORDS AND WORLDS THAT ARE TRUTHFUL AND TRUE

LUIZA PRADO DE O. MARTINS

A Red Path, A Black Sky

On August 23, 2019, an accident took place in the Rodovia Presidente Dutra, one of Rio de Janeiro's most important federal highways. In a section that cuts through the suburban municipality of Nova Iguaçu, a cargo truck carrying pesticide was hit by another vehicle. Vats rolled out of the truck, spilling their contents all along the highway, a bright pinkish-red liquid, dragged along the pavement by the wheels of other cars for hundreds of meters. The highway was temporarily closed as the liquid, considered harmful to humans, was cleaned up. RJTV, the region's most popular midday news program, aired footage of workers in hazmat suits shoveling the dried remains of the substance into large white bags under the cheerful headline 'Colorful Dutra'.[1] The exact nature of the pesticide, as well as the name of the company or companies responsible for its manufacturing and transportation, went unmentioned. The ensuing traffic jams slowed the flow of vehicles from city center to periphery for kilometers.

Four days earlier, around 3 p.m. on August 19, 2019, day abruptly turned into darkness in São Paulo. The skies above the metropolis, so often obscured by rainy clouds, acquired an unusual, black-brown hue; a sooty curtain falling prematurely over the city's bewildered inhabitants. Later that afternoon, the thick clouds finally released their cargo – a deep black rain, heavy with the unexpected scent of smoke.[2] The reason for this dark rain did not take much guessing: the fires devouring the Amazon rainforest along Brazil's northernmost states had been in the news for a while. This was just one repercussion, finally reaching the country's largest and wealthiest city, pushed by a cold wind. São Paulo's Tietê River – once a clean, living body of water – had long ago been reduced to a sludgy, foul-smelling mass; now it was the turn of the skies to fall.

Rainforests don't burn spontaneously; they must be intentionally set on fire. In July 2019, INPE (Brazil's National Institute for Space Research) reported an 88 percent increase in wildfires in the Amazon basin, compared to the same time frame in the previous year.[3] For centuries before this summer, forests had covered a great portion of the tropical areas of South America. The fires that preceded the black rain, the premature nightfall, and the spillage of pesticides

---

1   Ana Luíza Guimarães, Globoplay, 'Acidente Derruba Agrotóxico Na Marginal Da Rodovia Na Baixada' (24 August 2019), https://globoplay.globo.com/v/7867648/.

2   Patrícia Figueiredo, 'Moradores de SP Coletam Água Preta de Chuva Em Dia Que a Cidade Ficou Sob Nuvem Escura', *G1* (20 August 2019), https://g1.globo.com/sp/sao-paulo/noticia/2019/08/20/moradores-de-sp-coletam-agua-preta-de-chuva-em-dia-que-a-cidade-ficou-sob-nuvem-escura.ghtml.

3   Ana Carolina Moreno, 'Desmatamento na Amazônia em junho é 88% maior do que no mesmo período de 2018', *G1* (3 July 2019), https://g1.globo.com/natureza/noticia/2019/07/03/desmatamento-na-amazonia-em-junho-e-88percent-maior-do-que-no-mesmo-periodo-de-2018.ghtml.

had, in truth, been consuming everything in their path since European ships first arrived on the shores of the continent. These events were part of an old tragedy, a long-festering wound. To consume, to devour until nothing is left — these practices are interwoven throughout the history of coloniality into the present, from the foodstuffs taken from the Americas to be served to eager Europeans, to the voracious consumption of living black and brown bodies at the table of colonial economy, to the ravenous devouring of the Earth itself in the quest for endless economic growth. Avidity, in short, which leads inevitably to destruction; rapacity, which hinges on a vastly unequal distribution of the conditions necessary for well-being.

It is this hunger that underscores the rhetoric of exploitation of human and nonhuman beings at the root of the current climate crisis; a hunger that classifies not only forests, valleys, lakes, and seas, but also some people, as 'resources'. In his book *Ideias para adiar o fim do mundo* (Ideas to Postpone the End of the World), Indigenous writer and activist Ailton Krenak remarks that '[w]hen we remove the personhood from the river, the mountain, when we remove their senses, thinking that this is an exclusively human attribute, we allow these places to become residues of extractivist industrial activity.'[4] He points out: 'If there is an eagerness to consume nature, there is also one to consume subjectivities — our subjectivities.'[5] While some continue to devour, consuming with ferocious greed, others are starved by scarcity.

This is, of course, a produced scarcity, constructed through a mechanism that negates the personhood of some subjects, human and nonhuman, to classify them as exploitable resources and consume them indiscriminately in the name of Western and capitalist notions of development. As soon as the human bodies exploited within this cycle cease to work in its favor, perhaps due to disease, hunger, conflict, or death; as soon as the material repercussions of this process emerge (food shortages, water contamination, an increase in global temperature, natural disasters), scarcity is declared. There is now not enough food and water for all; there are not enough natural resources to sustain so many living, breathing human bodies. Krenak asks, pointedly: 'Natural resources for whom? Sustainable development for what? What is there to sustain?'[6] The foundations of coloniality and capitalism have always hinged on this construction of scarcity: in order for wealth to exist, so too must poverty. In order for some to live, some must die. In order for some to be satisfied, others must be eaten. Although produced through a complex network of power relations, scarcity has become a defining, tangible circumstance in the lives of those on the margins of a world still scarred by colonial wounds; a world where the sky blackens and falls, and paths are painted toxic red. The imagined isn't imaginary.

There Is No Room

The narrative of scarcity needs a corresponding one — that of excess, directed at those whose bodies and lives are framed as exploitable resources in the quest for the accumulation of

---

4   Ailton Krenak, *Ideias para adiar o fim do mundo*, vol. 1, São Paulo: Companhia das Letras, 2019, p. 49.
     All quotes from this work, translation mine.
5   Krenak, *Ideias para adiar o fim do mundo*, p. 32.
6   Krenak, *Ideias para adiar o fim do mundo*, p. 22.

wealth through endless economic growth. The people for whom food, water, land, shelter, care, affection, and dignity will not be afforded. On July 11, 2017, BBC host Victoria Derbyshire interviewed philanthropist Melinda Gates and the United Kingdom Secretary of State for International Development at the time, Priti Patel, on her #VictoriaLIVE segment. The topic of discussion was birth control, particularly the initiatives led in the Global South by the Gates Foundation (co-chaired by the philanthropist and Patel's husband) and the UK government.

Birth control, Gates and Patel stressed, is a pivotal issue for fighting poverty in the Global South, for it allows women in these regions to continue their education, contribute to the local economy, and better provide for smaller, planned families. The programs initiated by the Gates Foundation are necessary, Gates argued, in order to address the conditions brought about by a 'population bulge' that has, in her words, caused the 'biggest population of adolescents we've ever had in the history of the Earth' to be currently 'coming through the developing world.' If denied access to birth control, this population will be condemned to a 'life of destitute poverty', she continued, whereas 'if you can offer a girl contraceptives, she will stay in school.' Patel additionally asserted that population growth in the 'developing world' doesn't only have a negative impact on local economies, it also puts undue pressure on the United Kingdom's resources and, more importantly, leads to increases in the flow of migrants to the country.[7]

The rhetoric employed by Gates and Patel, which positions poverty and scarcity as a direct result of population growth, dates back centuries. In 1798, British scholar Thomas Malthus published *An Essay on the Principles of Population*. In it, he argues that the while a nation's ability to produce food could increase arithmetically, its populace would grow exponentially, leading to a destructive cycle that would culminate in what is known as a Malthusian catastrophe. He writes:

> The power of population is so superior to the power of the earth to produce subsistence for man, that premature death must in some shape or other visit the human race. The vices of mankind are active and able ministers of depopulation. They are the precursors in the great army of destruction, and often finish the dreadful work themselves. But should they fail in this war of extermination, sickly seasons, epidemics, pestilence, and plague advance in terrific array, and sweep off their thousands and tens of thousands. Should success be still incomplete, gigantic inevitable famine stalks in the rear, and with one mighty blow levels the population with the food of the world.[8]

Though not the first to propose these ideas, Malthus remains their most famous advocate. Anthropologist Eric Ross notes that Malthusian theories have been fundamental 'to provide an enduring argument for the prevention of social and economic change and to obscure, in both academic and popular thinking, the real roots of poverty, inequality and environmental

---

7   Victoria Derbyshire, BBC News (9 a.m.–11 a.m. 11 July 2017), http://archive.org/details/
     BBCNEWS_20170711_080000_Victoria_Derbyshire.
8   Thomas Robert Malthus, *An Essay on the Principle of Population*, CreateSpace Independent Publishing
     Platform, 2014 (1798), p. 50.

deterioration.'[9] Through the Malthusian lens, scarcity is not an inevitable – and desired – outcome of capitalist systems, but rather a result of the actions and choices of the poor.[10] Since Malthus's initial formulation, his arguments have been periodically revisited and recycled by academics and activists alike, from Paul Ehrlich (one of the first biologists to blame environmental collapse on overpopulation)[11] to Margaret Sanger, whose crusade for the right to birth control in the early 20th century was animated by the perception that many of the problems that afflicted poor women were results of unregulated fertility.[12]

Scholars Kalpana Wilson and Laura Briggs stress, however, that population control policies implemented in the Global South, which are underscored by Neo-Malthusian beliefs and advanced with the financial and political incentives of Northern nations, need to be understood as continuations of the colonial/imperial project, in that they pathologize the sex and reproduction of colonial subjects for the benefit of colonizers.[13] Interventions on the fertility and sexuality of colonial subjects are thus framed as necessary and beneficial. In the rhetoric of humanitarian aid presented by Patel and Gates, they are described as strategies for the empowerment of women and girls, devised to effectively introduce this demographic into the (low-paid) workforce of the Global South. Although both interviewees specifically used the designation 'developing countries' to politically and geographically position the subjects of the policies and programs they discuss, this designation obfuscates the complexity and diversity of the colonial subjects whose sexualities and fertilities are matters of such scrutiny. As a result, this designation also obscures the ways in which population control policies have been fundamental for the preservation of colonial racial hierarchies in the United States, as has been thoroughly documented and discussed by scholars such as Dorothy Roberts,[14] Angela Davis,[15] Elena Gutiérrez,[16] and Anne Hendrixson.[17] Patel's argument, in particular, aligns itself with the discourse associating population growth in the Global South with threats to national identity and security, identified by Hendrixson as a fundamental rationale behind US – and, I would expand, Western – military interventionism in the Middle East, and the surveillance of Muslims and Arabs circulating within US and European borders.

9   Eric B. Ross, *The Malthus Factor: Poverty, Politics and Population in Capitalist Development*, New York: Zed Books, 1998, p. 1.
10   Kalpana Wilson, *Race, Racism and Development: Interrogating History, Discourse and Practice*, New York: Zed Books, 2012.
11   Paul R. Ehrlich, *The Population Bomb*, New York: Ballantine Books, 1969.
12   Dorothy Roberts, *Killing the Black Body: Race, Reproduction, and the Meaning of Liberty*, New York: Vintage Books, 1998.
13   Wilson, *Race, Racism and Development*; Laura Briggs, *Reproducing Empire: Race, Sex, Science, and U.S. Imperialism in Puerto Rico*, Berkeley: University of California Press, 2002.
14   Dorothy Roberts, *Killing the Black Body*.
15   Angela Y. Davis, *Women, Race, & Class*, New York: Vintage, 1983.
16   Elena R. Gutiérrez, *Fertile Matters: The Politics of Mexican-Origin Women's Reproduction*, Austin: University of Texas Press, 2008.
17   Anne Hendrixson, 'Angry Young Men, Veiled Young Women: Constructing a New Population Threat', *The Corner House*, Briefing 34 (2 December 2004), http://www.thecornerhouse.org.uk/resource/angry-young-men-veiled-young-women.

The works of Wilson and Briggs focus primarily on how organizations and institutions based in the US or Europe promote these policies in the Global South; a similar racist logic, however, also governs healthcare initiatives deployed by many institutions and organizations within the Global South, directed at locally marginalized communities. The systematic, nonconsensual, mass sterilization of Indigenous peoples in Peru during the regime of dictator Alberto Fujimori in the 1990s is one such instance.[18] In Brazil, anthropologist Emilia Sanabria documented the widespread and coercive administration of the birth-control shot Depo-Provera to low-income women who resort to government-funded family planning services in the city of Salvador.[19] Current Brazilian President Jair Bolsonaro has long publicly supported many of Fujimori's ideas, defending strict population control policies aimed at the country's poorest as a way to 'control criminality and poverty.'[20] Bolsonaro's rhetoric is far from unique: historically, population control policies have been presented in Brazil as carrying positive economic implications for the general population,[21] a strategy to ward off the impending threat of scarcity.

Further complicating this scenario, as conversations on the climate crisis and its current and future impacts gain more prominence, concerns over possible connections between overpopulation, the increase of global temperatures, and fears of widespread scarcity have been placed once again in the spotlight – to the point that acts of white supremacist violence have been animated by the fear of a looming climactic disaster triggered by the presence of brown and black people within the borders of Western nations.[22] The idea of bodies in excessive abundance is inseparable from the colonial structures that have long sought to classify humans into hierarchical categories. Rhetoric becomes fear becomes policy becomes violence becomes rhetoric; a process woven into the everyday lives of those who, although they 'hold on to this Earth, are those who are forgotten along the borders of the planet, the margins of rivers, the shores of oceans, in Africa, in Asia, or in Latin America.'[23] Though critical of the 'population bomb' rhetoric, in her contribution to the book *Making Kin Not Population*, Donna Haraway circles around the discourse of scarcity related to the climate crisis, arguing that:

18   *A Woman's Womb* (dir. Mathilde Damoisel, 2010), downloadable at: http://www.cultureunplugged.com/play/4623/A-Woman-s-Womb.
19   Emilia Sanabria, *Plastic Bodies: Sex Hormones and Menstrual Suppression in Brazil*, Durham: Duke University Press, 2016.
20   Ranier Bragon, 'Bolsonaro defendeu esterilização de pobres para combater miséria e crime', *Folha de S.Paulo* (11 June 2018), https://www1.folha.uol.com.br/poder/2018/06/bolsonaro-defendeu-esterilizacao-de-pobres-para-combater-miseria-e-crime.shtml.
21   Sanabria, *Plastic Bodies*; Lilia Moritz Schwarcz, 'Espetáculo da miscigenação', *Estudos Avançados* 8.20 (April 1994): 137-152.
22   Natasha Lennard, 'The El Paso Shooter Embraced Eco-Fascism. We Can't Let the Far Right Co-Opt the Environmental Struggle', *The Intercept* (5 August 2019), https://theintercept.com/2019/08/05/el-paso-shooting-eco-fascism-migration/.
23   Krenak, *Ideias para adiar o fim do mundo*, p. 21.

Food production is a major contributor to climate change and the extinction crisis, with, as usual, those humans and nonhumans benefitting most suffering the least dire impacts. The super-peopling of the earth with both humans and industrial and pathogenic nonhumans is a worlding practice premised on the commitment to endless growth and vastly unequal well-being.[24]

Although in this passage Haraway does leave room for a critique that focuses on the systems and networks that construct scarcity within capitalism, she later recants this line, writing that 'blaming Capitalism, Imperialism, Neoliberalism, Modernization, or some other "not us" for ongoing destruction webbed with human numbers will not work.'[25] Additionally, she maintains that 'anti-racist feminist avoidance of thinking and acting in public about the pressing urgencies of human and nonhuman global populations is akin to the denial of anthropogenic climate change by some deeply believing US Christians',[26] and goes so far as to 'only half-jokingly call for a sliding scale approach to global reduction of human numbers.'[27] Under this system, she suggests, those willing to birth a human baby would need to collect tokens from other prospective parents; the number of necessary tokens would vary according to the parents' cultural, economic, racial, and ethnic background. Haraway's argument fails to consider that not all humans relate to the Earth in the same way; while she does admit that those living in so-called developed Western societies might impact the planet differently from people living in other societal organizations, this admission does not make its way into the core logic of her argument. Let us return again to Krenak, who remarks:

If we imprinted upon the planet Earth a mark so heavy that it characterizes an era, which may remain even after we are no longer here, because we are exhausting the sources of life that allow us to prosper and feel that we are home [...] it is because we are again in front of a dilemma I have already alluded to: we exclude from life, locally, the forms of organization that are not integrated to the world of commodities, risking all other forms of living – at least the ones we thought of as possible, where there was co-responsibility to the places we live and the respect for the life of beings, and not only this abstraction we allowed ourselves to construct as one humanity, which excludes all others and other beings.[28]

While Haraway insists this system would not be imposed but rather willingly embraced, her speculative proposal relies on the assumption of good will from all involved. Five hundred years of history have, however, abundantly shown this is not the case. As long as some people are perceived as not fully human, any such system is bound to facilitate violence being inflicted upon already marginalized populations – those living at the blunt end of what philosopher Maria Lugones calls the colonial/modern gender system. This system, Lugones clarifies, is fundamental to the establishment and continuation of the colonial project, and

---

24 Adele Clarke and Donna J. Haraway (eds), *Making Kin not Population: Reconceiving Generations*, Chicago: Prickly Paradigm Press, 2018, pp. 71-72.
25 Clarke and Haraway (eds), *Making Kin not Population*, p. 88.
26 Clarke and Haraway (eds), *Making Kin not Population*, p. 87.
27 Clarke and Haraway (eds), *Making Kin not Population*, p. 75.
28 Krenak, *Ideias para adiar o fim do mundo*, pp. 46-47.

includes what she calls a 'light' and a 'dark' side which operate in distinct ways, and act upon distinct bodies. Hegemonic (that is, European) constructions of gender and sex/sexuality are characteristic of the 'light' side of the colonial/modern gender system, which orders 'the lives of white bourgeois men and women'.[29] Concurrently, this light side constructs the meaning (epistemological and ontological) of the modern categories of 'men' and 'women'.[30]

The 'dark' side to the colonial/modern gender system governs the lives of those who exist outside of white bourgeois heteropatriarchy. Both sides of this gender system are violent, yet they manifest this inherent violence in different ways. Whereas white women are encumbered with perpetuating the white race – as Angela Davis has also highlighted[31] – women of color are 'understood as animals in the deep sense of "without gender", sexually marked as female, but without the characteristics of femininity.'[32] In the rhetoric of harm reduction related to the climate crisis, similar arguments are translated into calls for the surveillance of fertility – many similar to Haraway's – framed as necessary and beneficial for the entire world's population. Concurrently, the uncomfortable fact of the Global North's perpetual hunger for disposable goods, exploitable bodies, and natural resources – all key factors in the ongoing crisis – often remains un- or under-examined. Instead the blame is shifted to those existing under the duress inflicted through centuries of colonial domination, which as Krenak stresses, is in itself an ongoing project of world-ending.[33] Ultimately, these concerns reveal the perversity of calls for care – reproductive care, in particular – that do not adequately address underlying capitalist-colonial articulations. This in itself is a violence, one more way of consuming an 'other'.

Predictably, the narrative of climate crisis linked to uncontrolled reproduction is materialized in technologies currently being developed to provide so-called solutions to the perceived problem of overpopulation. A notable example is that of the startup Microchips Biotech, backed by the Gates Foundation and partnered with Israeli company Teva Pharmaceutical, whose flagship product, announced in 2014, is a remote-controlled smart birth-control implant that had been planned for commercial release in 2018.[34] The microchip can be turned on and off with a proprietary app controlled by a physician; it is designed to work for up to sixteen years – so for a large part of one's fertile life – as opposed to the three years of existing contraceptive implants. Additionally, the implant could collect a number of data points about patients, ostensibly to provide tailored healthcare solutions. The chip, Bill Gates clarified in 2014, was being conceived with the developing world in mind, more so than Western audiences, the rationale being that in these regions, it would mean a 'form

29   Maria Lugones, 'Heterosexualism and the Colonial/Modern Gender System', *Hypatia* 22.1 (2007): 186-209, p.206.
30   Lugones, 'Heterosexualism'.
31   Davis, *Women, Race, & Class*, p. 209.
32   Lugones, 'Heterosexualism', p. 202.
33   Krenak, *Ideias para adiar o fim do mundo*.
34   Microchips Biotech, http://microchipsbiotech.com/; Rob Matheson, 'Major Step for Implantable Drug-Delivery Device', *MIT News* (29 June 2015), http://news.mit.edu/2015/implantable-drug-delivery-microchip-device-0629.

of reproductive justice', rather than merely a 'lifestyle choice',[35] and could be distributed as part of the numerous birth-control programs initiated by the foundation in the Global South. As of 2019, no new information has been publicly released about the project.

The mass distribution of devices like the Microchips implant could have serious implications for the digitalized biometric surveillance of those living on the 'dark side' of the colonial/ modern gender system. These bodies have long been hypervisible, targets of surveillance by public and private actors. In order to understand the wide-ranging implications of this surveillance, however, it is fundamental to approach 'reproduction' as a broader set of life-making practices and articulations, rather than as a strictly biological process. Returning to the question of scarcity helps reframe the oft-repeated narrative of 'choice' pushed by many white Western feminists in relation to reproduction. Scarcity – of food, housing, healthcare, education, adequate climactic conditions – is precisely the argument that animates much of the supposed necessity for contraceptive technologies such as the one developed by Microchips Biotech in the Global South and so insistently pushed by the likes of Gates and Patel. It follows that in order to avoid scarcity, these subjects then must be monitored, their fertility controlled 'for their own good', considered incapable of making such decisions on their own. So goes the perverse narrative of 'care' tied to scarcity: the vulnerable must accept and be grateful for any apparent help provided by the same powerful actors who profit from that vulnerability in the first place.

It is also fundamental to consider that the lived experience of constructed scarcity has profound effects on the paths and choices one feels compelled to follow. In 18th century Surinam, naturalist Maria Sibylla Merian documented the use of an infusion of peacock flower by enslaved Indigenous and African peoples as a way to provoke abortions. This, Merian stressed, was a reaction to the conditions of extreme violence to which these people were subjected; they did so, she wrote, 'so that their children will not become slaves like they are.'[36] Currently, although the threat of climate disasters looms over the entire planet, there is still a sharp distinction between those most affected, and those who command the resources to survive the oncoming catastrophe. The dominant narrative of the climate crisis is one of suffering delegated to someone else, somewhere else by an economic system that hinges on the production of scarcity for some in order to offer wealth for others. It is a narrative that negates the personhood of beings: human and nonhuman, living and not yet or no longer embodied – a lingering effect of the colonial hierarchies that have long been used to justify the expropriation of land, exploitation of bodies, and extraction of so-called resources. It is a narrative that feeds the colonial hunger for homogenization and globalization, which seeks to 'suppress diversity, deny the plurality of forms of life, existence, and habits', offering 'the same menu, the same costumes and, if possible, the same language to all.'[37] And so those who 'hold on to this Earth' are pushed and shoved into a monocultural, universalizing narrative,

35   Dominic Basulto, 'This Amazing Remote-Controlled Contraceptive Microchip You Implant under Your Skin Is the Future of Medicine', *Washington Post* (17 July 2014), https://www.washingtonpost.com/ news/innovations/wp/2014/07/17/this-amazing-remote-controlled-contraceptive-microchip-you-implant-under-your-skin-is-the-future-of-medicine/?utm_term=.7e8bcf013438.
36   Maria Sibylla Merian, *Metamorphosis Insectorum Surinamensium*, Tielt: Lannoo Publishers, 2016, p. 45.
37   Krenak, *Ideias para adiar o fim do mundo*, pp. 22-23.

while simultaneously remaining 'forgotten along the borders of the planet, the margins of rivers, the shores of oceans',[38] navigating the same perverse plot that produced and produces this marginalization. When dark skies loom above, however, Krenak reminds us: 'There are so many small constellations of people scattered all over the world who dance, sing, make rain.'[39] World-endings have happened so many times before, marking the margins of the world like scars, but 'when you feel the sky is getting too low, all you have to do is to push it back and breathe.'[40]

An Abundance of Small Gestures

How is it possible, then, to create the conditions for life within a political system designed to produce death? How to counteract a narrative of scarcity for which the only resolution presented by the current system is the total consumption of the Earth, and with it all of the persons – human and nonhuman, living and not yet or no longer embodied – who exist in relation to it? How to sustain radical, decolonizing practices of care and affect that directly challenge the infrastructures that monitor and restrict the ability to create futures and sustain worlds that are multiple, plural, heterogenous?

In 2019, I undertook a joint residency between transmediale and the Universität der Künste Berlin to work on a project titled 'The Councils of the Pluriversal: Affective Temporalities of Reproduction and Climate Change'. In it, I intended to convene the Councils – a series of meetings with activists, artists, elders, and thinkers hailing from marginalized groups in Northern nations, and the Global South. In these events I would propose discussions pertaining to the entanglements between the climate crisis, reproduction, ancestral and future histories, land and belonging, and radical, decolonizing forms of care. A guiding principle to these events would be the notion of '*un mundo donde quepan muchos mundos*' – that is, a world in which many worlds fit – a conception first advanced by the Zapatista liberation movement in Mexico:

> Many words are walked in the world. Many worlds are made. Many worlds make us. There are words and worlds that are lies and injustices. There are words and worlds that are truthful and true. We make truthful worlds. We are made by truthful words. In the world of the powerful there is space only for the big and their servants. In the world we want there is space for all. The world we want is a world where many worlds fit. The nation we build is one that may fit all the peoples and their languages, that may be walked by all gaits, that may be laughed in, that may be awoken.[41]

This conception rejects universalizing impulses toward consensus, favoring instead temporal, spatial, and infrastructural multiplicities that nurture the emergence of

38 Krenak, *Ideias para adiar o fim do mundo*, p. 21.
39 Krenak, *Ideias para adiar o fim do mundo*, p. 26.
40 Krenak, *Ideias para adiar o fim do mundo*, p. 28.
41 Comité Clandestino Revolucionario Indígena-Comandancia General del Ejército Zapatista de Liberación Nacional, 'Cuarta Declarión de la Selva Lacandona', *Enlace Zapatista*, http://enlacezapatista.ezln.org.mx/1996/01/01/cuarta-declaracion-de-la-selva-lacandona/. Translation mine.

epistemological and ontological complexity. 'The Councils of the Pluriversal' were conceived as dialogic and idiosyncratic events, not meant to provide exhaustive, unifying, or definitive summaries of issues of care, temporalities, reproduction, and climate change, but rather to provide possible points of entry to think and act through these issues.

Throughout the research process, I had the honor and privilege to strengthen and expand affective bonds of care and intimacy with a number of people operating within the vastly distinct contexts of Rio de Janeiro and Boa Vista, Brazil, and Berlin, Germany. I extend my deepest gratitude to Dagmar Schultz and Ika Hügel-Marshall in Berlin; to Vó Bernaldina, Jaider Esbell, Paula Berbert, Raquel Blaque, Amazoner Arawak, Parmênio Citó, and Caio Clímaco in Boa Vista; as well as to the hundreds of activists I encountered in the streets of Rio, protesting while caring for one another, and keeping each other safe. These bonds were not all started as part of this project; most were existing relationships that had emerged through shared interests in the struggle for decolonization, as well as for reproductive and climate justice. Some of these bonds extended, too, to nonhuman beings – the *lavrado* vegetation, the rivers and *igarapés* of the state of Roraima, where Boa Vista is located[42] – as well as to human beings no longer embodied – in particular, to Audre Lorde and May Ayim, whose truth in words and worlds is capable of transcending life itself.

Most importantly, all of these persons were already, through their practices – as activists, artists, curators, singers, cooks, storytellers, cultural workers, writers, poets, filmmakers, educators, and care workers, among others – conducting their own versions of what I had come to call 'The Councils of the Pluriversal'. Amongst all of the experiences I had while developing this research, this was perhaps the most significant and humbling realization: art, particularly politically oriented art, often risks gravitating toward grand, sensational gestures. These become performances that benefit those who hold power, including artists themselves, far more than those actually affected by the issues at hand.

There was no need for me to name the Councils as such; they already existed in alternate forms, practiced by people whose sincerity, commitment, and deep understanding of their communities and peers allow them to articulate spaces where ever-evolving forms of caring for one another can emerge across an extended period of time. This type of maintenance work is made of smaller gestures with long-term repercussions, gestures that trouble the narrative of scarcity advanced by capitalism, and point toward other possibilities, other realities, other worlds where abundance – of time, generosity, affection, patience – is possible. This work is Makuxi elder Vó Bernaldina preparing *damurida*, an ancestral fish stew made with local ingredients, cooked in a pot made with clay borrowed from the land, and eaten with cassava flour, for those who arrive to visit artist Jaider Esbell's gallery in Boa Vista. It is artist and cook Raquel Blaque repurposing the leftovers with foraged local herbs and vegetables to feed a group of school students who wanted a space where they could engage with Indigenous art, and discuss the ongoing fires that consumed the forest south of Boa Vista. It is artist and anthropologist Amazoner Arawak sharing stories on Wapixana cosmologies, and the

---

42   *Lavrado*, a Brazilian savanna; *igarapé*, an Amazonian watercourse.

exploitation of Indigenous material cultures by European cultural institutions over a bottle of *caxiri*.[43] It is Jaider's generosity in opening up his life, his gallery, his home to those who arrive in Boa Vista with the intent to live and exchange and learn. It is a group of young students holding a large placard protesting the burning of the Amazon in Rio de Janeiro and being fed by their peers, so that they wouldn't need to drop the sign. It is Dagmar Schultz and Ika Hügel-Marshall, lifelong friends of Audre Lorde, cooking a meal in their home to introduce young feminist, anti-racist, and environmental activists to one another – in the same way Lorde did, too. It is Vó Bernaldina singing a Makuxi song celebrating the recognition of the Raposa Serra do Sol territory as Indigenous land.

Developing bonds of affection is a long-term process, as remarked by Ailton Krenak to art worker and cultural producer Paula Berbert and relayed to me in conversation. It is only through nurturing sincere, solid relationships that the conditions for sustaining life can emerge; that truly pluriversal modes of engaging with each other and with the world can come into being. Counteracting the narrative of scarcity demands abundance. In the end, instead of convening councils as I had imagined, the main avenue of work became an exploration of these different forms of relating and practicing care with other bodies, human and nonhuman; the beginning of a long-term engagement, whose first ramifications will be presented at transmediale 2020. After all, as Krenak points out:

> Why does the feeling of falling cause us such discomfort? We haven't done anything lately but fall. Fall, fall, fall. So why are we worried about the process of falling? Let us use all of our critical and creative capacity to build colorful parachutes. Let us think of space not as a confined place, but as a cosmos where we can fall with colorful parachutes.[44]

Decolonization is not an individual choice; it demands collective, sustained, committed work. Let us feed these visions for a future of blue skies and open paths. Let us nourish each other with responsibility, care, affection, and patience.

---

43   A fermented cassava-based drink, typical of the Amazon basin.
44   Krenak, *Ideias para adiar o fim do mundo*, p. 30.

HUMAN, NONHUMAN AND NETWORKS IN BETWEEN

NETWORK TOPOLOGIES: FROM THE EARLY WEB TO HUMAN MESH NETWORKS

Alessandro Ludovico

NETWORK TOPOLOGIES: FROM THE EARLY WEB TO HUMAN MESH NETWORKS

ALESSANDRO LUDOVICO

Network as a Paradigm, Network as a System

We live in a space of networks. The connections between people, data, spaces, and objects have become more apparent and even assumed thanks to the infrastructure that manifests its pulsating presence through our screens and LED-equipped devices. Yet despite their prevalence, how can we assign networks an adequately general definition that would be cross-disciplinary? Here's one attempt to compose such a definition from various scientific and cultural domains: 'elements, nodes, or sub-units connected as a whole.' The 'whole' defines the total networked space, even in its potential size and shape, which is perhaps the most ungraspable element of the contemporary moment, thanks to the average network's dimension and complexity. Its parts determine the individuality of its essential components, the nodes.

The space we inhabit is filled with mostly opaque active nodes (such as our devices), largely at a low hierarchy in the global grid of interconnections, which privileges centralized entities being in control of all the peripheral ones, and whose production and infrastructural use is ascribable to a relatively small number of online and hardware companies. Nonetheless, given that each node is individual, there remains an autonomous capacity to conceptually redefine networks and create sub- or separated networks at will. Using the same technical infrastructure, we can connect with peers on almost infinite nodes that are just a few steps away, while escaping the official 'grids'.

The network structure must first be acknowledged as an abstract system, and second as a manifestation of an enormous implementation of information technology; as a paradigm, which reframes the technical structure as a conceptual model. In this text I will try to analyze the main changes in the evolution of network topologies through the past decades, in line with the experiments we have accomplished with *Neural* magazine over the same time frame. By 'network topology' I mean a blend of the mathematical and more general definition of topology, applied to networks, so something like: 'spatial relations, whose constituent parts are interrelated, unaffected by the continuous changes in shape, size, or nodes.' I will explore various embodiments of these topologies in the interplay of networked cultures, the networking practices of *Neural*, and the techno-cultural developments of networks.

Early Utopia: Revealed Topologies and Personal Networks

In the first decade of the public and then mass internet (early 90s to early 00s) the visualization of the network structure represented the new underlying digital structure that was forming behind the visual appearance of single pages (typically shown as browser content). The lack of any accurately compiled topologies, due to the constant growth and evolution of these rapidly expanding networks, resulted in the rapid obsolescence of any 'visual map' that tried to represent these network topologies. This inspired the first generation of net artists to develop their own visualizations, either fixed or dynamic, to express or create an overview of physically or conceptually interconnected nodes. The *Web Stalker* browser (1997) and JODI's *Map* (1999) are among the most celebrated of these net art works.

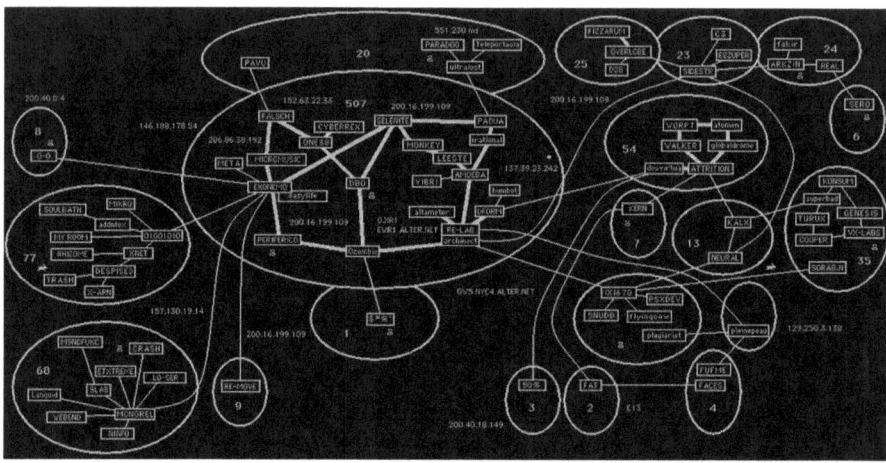

Fig. 1: JODI's Map (1999), http://map.jodi.org/.

The former, developed by I/O/D (Matthew Fuller, Colin Green, and Simon Pope), was a fully functioning alternative web browser whose main feature was visualizing the links connecting to the requested page. Fuller compared the dissection and rendering of the network to Gordon Matta Clark's 'Splitting' action (1974) where he literally bisected a whole house (already slated for demolition).[1] The *Web Stalker* generated an abstract map of connections, 'as a crawler function gradually moving through the network. We saw the logical structure of websites, established by the links, in and between them, as another key resource.'[2] Unveiling the infrastructure and relations of the network in this way, the *Web Stalker* was antithetical to the page-centered, accurate layout of other browsers. Net art critic Josephine Bosma writes that 'it embodies [...] art as a process.'[3] The browser was downloadable, and also distributed in other ways, like surreptitiously installed on office computers and passed, for example, via floppy disks during events, as I/O/D was also the name of a floppy-based publication by the trio, founded in 1994.

1   Matthew Fuller, *Behind the Blip. Essays on the Culture of Software*, Brooklyn, NY: Autonomedia, 2003, p. 40.

2   Matthew Fuller, 'Crawl, Map, Link, Read, Copy, Repeat', *Rhizome* (17 February 2017), https://rhizome.org/editorial/2017/feb/17/iod-4-web-stalker/.

3   Josephine Bosma, *Nettitudes: Let's Talk Net Art*, Rotterdam: NAi, 2011, p. 76.

JODI's iconic low-tech *Map* (http://map.jodi.org) has a different, subjective perspective, and was created by internet artist duo Joan Heemskerk and Dirk Paesmans. It was a clickable online network diagram representing the 'landscape of domains and sites that most interested them at the time', with subjective relationships.[4] JODI's *Map* accidentally formalized part of the net art avant-garde, and enlightened some of its obscure manifestations, such as the French PAVU collective, interested in détourning the web, and the fals.ch music/CD-ROM label. The *Map* diagrammatically compiles an interconnected visual 'document' which outlived the time and context of its making. In a way it was 'JODI's Internet', frozen in time and expressed through a curated selection of entities, all within net art circles. This selection both scaled down the network to which they were referring, to a size and shape that could be manageably represented, and restricted it to a sphere of mutual influence. (Incidentally, the earliest version of the *Neural* website was one of the nodes of the JODI's *Map*.)

Another couple of examples, developed to fill the gap between the imaginary around emerging networks and their actual structure, help to categorize different types of transparent network topologies further. Lisa Jevbratt's *1:1* (1999) was a database with 'the addresses of every Web site in the world and interfaces through which to view and use the database'.[5] The topology is represented through pixels which make lines and stripes with various attributed colors, abstracted in order to contain the 'whole' on one screen. As Rachel Greene describes, in Jevbratt's work 'a landscape emerges', which 'tends towards the imagistic and the representational.'[6]

Schoenerwissen/OfCD's *Minitasking* (2002), developed by Anne Pascual and Marcus Hauer, was, in the words of its makers, a 'graphical browser for surfing the Gnutella network.'[7] It visualized through different color bubbles the evolution of a query and the ongoing activity and size of the Servents. The topology of *Minitasking* represented the structure of the first decentralized peer-to-peer network, used for the exchange of mostly copyrighted files. The network was transparent in size and form, while the anonymity of the participants was still protected through the abstractions of the rendering. Compared to *1:1*, it shows how the topologies of autonomous and mostly functional networks must be constantly reshaped and their representations compellingly dynamic.

Somewhat ironically, a side effect of the dissemination of early mass computer virus attacks were visualizations of the network, as they made its topology transparent. At the peak of their infections, they could reveal large parts of global interconnections – and indeed, weaknesses. As I wrote in *Neural* in 2002, 'The more computers get infected (or in other words will accept the message), the bigger the impact and reaction on the network will be. The critical mass of data spread around the network, temporarily transforms the shape and the content of the network, so it varies its own conscience.'[8]

---

4   Alexander R. Galloway, 'Jodi's Infrastructure', *e-flux Journal* 74 (June 2016), https://www.e-flux.com/journal/74/59810/jodi-s-infrastructure/.

5   Lisa Jevbratt, 1999, http://128.111.69.4/~jevbratt/1_to_1/description.html.

6   Rachel Greene, *Internet Art*, London: Thames & Hudson, 2004, p. 140.

7   Schoenerwissen/OfCD, 'Minitasking', https://rhizome.org/art/artbase/artwork/minitasking/.

8   Alessandro Ludovico, 'Infection as Communication', *Neural* 22 (2002).

Yet another example of a transparent sub-network is the webring, a circular chain of shared interest websites, at once horizontal and sequential. This was the underlying construction of *Refresh* (1996), a net art work by Alexei Shulgin, Vuk Ćosić, and Andreas Broeckman, which showed how the connection between nodes required a negotiation among the peers. Ćosić describes the work as follows:

> The Refresh Project [...] was a collaborative online performance done in October of 1996 during the opening of the St. Petersburg Biennial. Alexei Shulgin, Andreas Broeckman and moi have decided to create a loop between web pages using the simple & stupid <refresh> tag. Then we arranged for an IRC session with anybody interested to participate and have slowly woven something like 25 different sites in one global ring.[9]

A floppy disk with a 'snapshot' of this work was then distributed on the cover of the third Nettime reader at the MetaForum III conference in Budapest that year – an offline sharing of the existence and topology of this network to other potential participants (and thereby nodes).

These works (with the exception of *1:1*) aimed to both autonomize and connect compatible nodes in independent sub-networks, transparent but protected, with the fascinating possibility of reconfiguring these same nodes in order to evolve their meaning and function. They can still be understood as what Hakim Bey (Peter Lamborn Wilson) defined in 1991 as 'temporary autonomous zones.'[10] A network ecology emerges from these practices, with some key elements: transparency, the creation of autonomous and negotiated sub-networks, the potential of interconnections and their temporary or stable reconfigurations and extensions, and the nodes and their respective roles.

Networking Practices: The Interdependent Networks of *Neural*

Pre-internet alternative and radical networks of communications share the figure of the 'networker': subjects developing their own networks, within or outside predefined structures. In mail art, this figure predominates, with the networker replacing the 'artist', with the prerogative to create networks of artistic production, public sharing, and archiving. In the words of Vittore Baroni, one of the most prominent figures in mail art: 'I saw the networker as a new cultural figure, a sort of meta-author who created contexts for collective expression rather than conventional individual works, and whose activities eluded the "vicious circle" of the art market and therefore needed new critical parameters and instruments to be fully analyzed and understood.'[11]

---

9   Ćosić, Vuk, '[-28] The Refresh Project', 2015, https://free.janezjansa.si/blog/2015/01/28-the-refresh-project/.

10   Hakim Bey, *T.A.Z: The Temporary Autonomous Zone, Ontological Anarchy, Poetic Terrorism*, New York: Autonomedia, 1991.

11   Vittore Baroni, 'Memo from a Networker', http://www.lomholtmailartarchive.dk/texts/vittore-baroni-memo-from-a-networker.

The networker here can be related to the privileged early internet scenario of relationships (small scale, quite unregulated, so mostly free and still technically simple), and to the practices of net art. The networker and early net artists share an underlying structure and principles, if not the scope and nature of their tools. For example, the Decentralized World-Wide Networker Congress for mail art in 1992 was a bottom-up structure of gatherings and events, creating and expanding upon sub-networks, including a three-day performance of eighty-six artists exchanging copy art via fax around the world.[12] Net artists meanwhile were creating dynamic sub-networks, performances, and initiatives globally, connected by the same spirit of distributed production, collaboration, and knowledge-sharing.

These practices all inspired *Neural* magazine, its production, economy, and associated activities. Founded in 1993, *Neural* began with one specific concept: to be a single node within a larger network of magazines and sources of information, all delivering content on digital culture, both investigating and expanding the established domains. The role of *Neural* has always been to weave together different data domains, in order to trigger a new awareness of digital culture and the growing network of entities producing this culture, which increasingly break the boundaries between fields of research.[13] Phillip Gochenour defined this approach as 'nodalism', which 'emphasizes the importance of links and connections and stigmatizes disconnectedness and solitude.'[14] This is not meant as a description of a condition, but a whole system: 'in a network model each unit, though different in itself, is part of an overall smoothly functioning system.'[15]

The *Neural* project has been built to echo the networks it nurtures and connects with, in a critical, but also open and collaborative way. Moreover, the development of a proper focused network has transcended the many platforms it occupies, and has entered into fruitful dialogues with other 'nodes'.[16] *Neural* took a few years to develop into a fully fledged informal network. In 2002, a network of magazines was cofounded, whose members could support each other in their publishing efforts, and discuss their shared condition, particularly the nodal relationship between online and offline publishing. The network was called Mag. net (magazine network of electronic cultural publishers) and involved thirteen international editors whose collective slogan became 'collaboration is better than competition', recursively reflecting its structure. Apart from sharing knowledge and developing projects among groups of members, three anthologies ('Mag.net Readers') were co-edited on the changing role of print and its ongoing mutation.

12   György Galántai, Júlia Klaniczay, and Kristine Stiles, *Artpool: The Experimental Art Archive of East-Central Europe; History of an Active Archive for Producing, Networking, Curating and Researching Art Since 1970*, Budapest: Artpool, 2013, p. 136.
13   Annette Wolfsberger, 'Interview with Alessandro Ludovico', in Nicola Mullenger and Annette Wolfsberger (eds) *Cultural Bloggers Interviewed*, Amsterdam: LabforCulture, 2010, pp. 69-80.
14   Phillip Gochenour, 'Nodalism', *Digital Humanities Quarterly* 5.3 (2011), http://www.digitalhumanities.org/dhq/vol/5/3/000105/000105.html.
15   Gochenour, 'Nodalism'.
16   Wolfsberger, 'Interview with Alessandro Ludovico'.

The mutual support network of Mag.net subsequently facilitated one of its members, Springerin editor Georg Schöllhammer, to curate 'Documenta 12 magazines' in Kassel in 2007, which involved almost one hundred independent art magazines from around the world. *Neural* contributed to this project, also developing relationships with some of the other featured publications, sharing similar conditions, interests, and attitudes.

In *Neural*'s publishing practice, another networked layer was developed a few years later, stemming from several experiments scattered in time. The infrastructure of distribution meant that our 500 or so subscribers included more than 150 institutional, mostly academic, libraries. These libraries could be thought of both as a preservation strategy for the magazine, hosting 'back-up' copies in distant places, and as a distribution strategy for art works embedded within the magazine. These art works, sometimes involving quite controversial ideological components, mostly consisted in artists' interventions into the space of the page, with or without extra materials added or attached. In this way the magazine became a limited-edition distribution platform, using the infrastructural network of library collections.

A further layer of the *Neural* project is the Neural Archive, which consists of the submissions and donations of publications the magazine has received over the last twenty-five years.[17] It is a searchable online catalogue of print media and art publications, and acts as a progressively growing representation of the community to which *Neural* magazine belongs – it is an archive of this community's production. In the near future, the Neural Archive may become connected with other similar archives, and already in itself shows the magazine's connections with the producers (publishers), and the inner connections among publications that emerge when you search all the issues. Music is not yet included in the archive, but could well be catalogued in the future, given our already established network of record labels and their contributions.

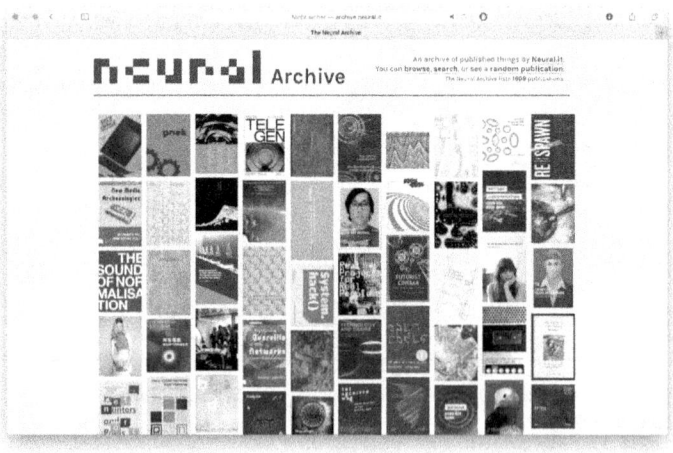

Fig.: Neural Archive, Screenshot.

17   The Neural Archive, http://archive.neural.it.

The funding of *Neural* is also 'networked', in that economic support for the project comes from a strategic network of subscribers, rather than from application-based funding, which *Neural* never applied for or received. From the beginning, a kind of crowdfund *ante litteram* was nurtured, with direct relations and communication that goes beyond the mere exchange of goods and money. On top of this, there's the community of reference, or the network of artists, curators, and institutions which periodically inform the magazine and/or are in dialogue about their productions.

All these intertwining networks support the publishing, artistic, and archiving practices, but they also need to be nourished. Their interconnection generates sometimes unpredictable positive effects – strategic information or support which resonates from one layer to another, and from one node to another, transversally – but this is only manageable as long as the size and complexity of the network is maintained within a certain scale. With one-to-one relationships between all the nodes, their incredible human capital – fueled by emotional as well as technological resources – can become too much at some point, and lead to dysfunctions and cracks.

What results is a cultural version of an 'interdependent network'. The nodes depend on each other for their ecology and economy. The technical term for these type of networks, 'cascading', highlights their fragility in case of failure, potentially causing breakdowns of the whole system.[18] However, when they are culturally constituted and mediated, the networks have a different structure, as the single parts are protected by their various roles, although still interdependent.

Such an interdependent network as we have built over time with *Neural* might represent a possible, hopeful model or strategy for managing our personal networks, preserving scale in direct relation to complexity, and creating long-term or short-term nurtured connections, instead of always looking for more – as is the pervasive commercial mantra.

The Opaque Topology of Social Media

While these kind of interdependent networks have a relatively transparent topology, at least in their public parts, in the case of *Neural*, the last revolution in communication we have seen, social media, is a self-transforming beast, which is less easy to discern. Social media platforms structurally hide their inner topology, all the while pushing for growth in the upper layer of users' connections, which boost profits, as a condition to thrive and survive. This process had already begun in the first decade of the world wide web, when the big players started to capitalize on the appropriation of the network topology, through indexes and search engines, or giving private space to host content, through 'portals'. The topology of networks became lucratively opaque and increasingly impenetrable.

---

18   Alessandro Vespignani, 'Complex Networks: The Fragility of Interdependency', *Nature* 464.7291 (April 2010): 984-985.

The early need and desire to be aware of the network topology has gradually shifted toward online corporations' need to include an ever larger number of users and content as assets, which has exploded with the social media paradigm and the 'appification' of everything, reiterated by most online platforms. This phenomenon is epitomized in the near total mediation of the economy of relationships, and so of networking, by social media. These platforms and protocols have triggered the largest voluntary creation of valuable and contextualized digital content, capitalizing on keeping their internal infrastructure hidden. It is an 'inclusive-exclusive' model: inclusive in terms of the functional accessibility of other users' data and connections (the capital of data), although dispossessing each user from their own data ownership; and exclusive insofar as the internal network is hidden and even adjusted by corporate technical and strategical algorithms (page rank, timeline order, etc.), which make any attempt to interpret or decode the model useless.

In this reality, the 'whole' topology is just too complex to map and detail, even at the level of single users with a relatively low threshold (or number of friends/followers/nodes): the user, pushed to increase his or her contacts/nodes, loses track of the 'whole' of their connections. The top-down inclusive-exclusive model works very well for the companies in this respect, handing management of the networks to the platform's owners.

It is nonetheless very important to interpret these networks. If in this model, technically 'conflict is non-functional', as Gochenour stated, then we can consider that social media stores an inordinate amount of useful contacts, which could become nodes of other focused networks, once identified and extrapolated from the corporate platform's rules.[19] Using the existing infrastructure of social media as a source of possible nodes of new independent, and even possibly interdependent networks, rather than number-driven platforms that encourage obsessive self-promotion, might trigger a different economy of networks and build new topologies.

Human Mesh Networks

It is important then to consider to build networks of connections creating meaning. With rising commercial attention on the amount of connections having an impact on self-confidence, building scaled-down networks, characterized primarily by the meaning of the exchange rather than the quantity of exchanged signals could dismantle the popularity paradigm. Indeed, if this paradigm evaluates the number of associations as capital, then we'd consider that 'the more connected, the more individualized a point is.'[20] The network is, as Latour affirms, a 'privileged mode of organization thanks to the very extension of information technology.'[21] It is a privilege to access infrastructures which reveal entities that could coalesce around specific ideas and projects, forming new independent networks and sub-networks, scaling down complexity through being aware of our networked topography, and enabling us to better

19   Gochenour, 'Nodalism'.
20   Bruno Latour, *Reassembling the Social: An Introduction to Actor-Network-Theory*, Oxford: Oxford University Press, 2008, p. 133.
21   Latour, *Reassembling the Social*, p. 129.

explore it. The six degrees of separation from the potential meaningful nodes should guide us toward finding the 'human capital' we want to cooperate with, escaping the sick dream of being either a hyperactive celebrity or a hyperactive audience. In this scenario, we'd value our discoverability in chosen contexts, in order to gain and pass on proximity from the nodes we want to build networks with, acting mostly outside the industrialized platforms. We should build 'human mesh networks' with interdependences that would preserve multiple potential layers of application and collectivity. The network topology of critical cultural forms embodies the concept of the network as a supportive infrastructure, a flexible skeleton for vital action. Networks are collective agents that author, facilitate, and propagate content, an essential part of the strategies necessary for instigating rebellion and alternative visions of society, for rethinking digital limits and conceptual possibilities. Once we reclaim the infrastructures, and a human scale supersedes technological complexity, we can start to properly shape our own networks with trusted nodes, making alliances between trusted entities of information with an open, non-self-rewarding attitude.

ANOTHER NET IS POSSIBLE

Rachel O'Dwyer

ANOTHER NET IS POSSIBLE

RACHEL O'DWYER

The term 'spectrum' describes the electromagnetic waves that are used to transmit everything: radio and television signals, cellular communications, and data from the Internet of Things. These waves are made of exactly the same stuff as the visible spectrum of light, but at frequencies invisible to humans. If you Google 'spectrum allocation chart', you'll see a range of color-coded maps showing how these frequencies are divided up: there are blocks for military operations, blocks for Bluetooth communications, blocks for 4G, blocks for emergency services, blocks for medical devices, and even blocks for garage-door openers. Ever since the Titanic sank in a mesh of competing radio signals, spectrum has been owned by governments and controlled by national regulators. With the exception of a small set of frequencies that are allocated for unlicensed uses, such as Wi-Fi and Bluetooth, licenses for the use of the remaining frequencies are either allocated to public resources such as national radio broadcasters, or auctioned, at exorbitant prices, to network operators. And as, in recent years, the potential for monetizing wireless communications has continued expanding – 5G, contextual advertisements, virtual reality gaming, fine-tuned logistics and mobile payments – the issue of spectrum ownership has come to the fore: Is public or private ownership the best way to manage wireless communications, or should spectrum be a common resource to which everyone has access, provided they follow some basic rules?

Ever since radio amateurs built their own crystal sets and surfed the shortwaves, the history of wireless has been ghosted by alternative practices that have challenged the ownership and control of spectrum. Ham-, micro-, and pirate-radio community members cobbled sets together from everyday domestic items, and experimented with Morse, voice, and, later, packet radio, to share communications and images in a sort of proto-internet.[1] Later, after the opening-up to experimentation of the ISM (industrial, scientific, and medical) bands, and the development of the 802.11 protocol,[2] Wi-Fi too became a contested space, with calls for a wireless commons to be built, using open spectrum. Network activists were particularly excited by Wi-Fi as a space where users could experiment with the collectively managing communications, outside of both the state and the market. Some of the best examples include guifi.net, a community wireless network in Catalonia and Spain that currently includes more than 27,000 operational nodes, and initiatives such as the Consume Network in London (now closed), NYC Mesh in the United States, and Freifunk in Berlin, to name just a few. Much was also made of 'war-driving' and 'war-chalking' practices, wherein activists allegedly used aesthetic forms of mapping to mark the existence in public spaces of open and closed

1   See for example, Susan J. Douglas, *Inventing American Broadcasting, 1899-1922*, Baltimore, London: Johns Hopkins University Press, 1987; and early accounts of amateur radio activities in The Marconigram, later Wireless World, which featured a regular supplement on set construction and technical assistance for enthusiasts.

2   IEEE 802.11 is part of a set of Local Access Network protocols used for implementing wireless local access networks (WLANs) in frequencies including the 2, GhZ and 5GhZ bands. The base version of the standard was released in 1997 and subsequently formed the foundation protocol for Wi-Fi network products.

wireless nodes.[3] Communities such as these advocated for a spectrum commons, through declarations such as 'The Wireless Commons Manifesto',[4] and worked to develop blueprints for cooperation; including via the application of some of the basic principles of Nobel Prize-winner Elinor Ostrom's work on common-pool resource management,[5] and the development of extra-legal agreements such as the FONN Compact, the Pico Peering Agreement, and the Network Commons License.[6] In time, innovations in Voice over Internet Protocol (VoIP), and hardware 'virtualization' (creating virtual versions of extremely costly cellular infrastructure such as base stations), pushed forward the development of not only open-source and community Wi-Fi networks, but also of open-source cellular networks.[7]

The Limitations of Networks

With the exception of large-scale projects such as guifi.net, community wireless networks have come to feel like a niche pursuit — an activity which was prominent in the golden age of Wi-Fi but which never gained traction. In the face of contemporary network politics, monolithic platforms, and large infrastructural rollout, it's hard to stay optimistic about such practices. While this article acknowledges the limitations of community wireless networks, it also explores their demands for, and experiments with, different models of ownership and cooperativism, arguing that these have never been more important than they are now. So, too, that certain elements of their practices — in imagining, inventing, resisting — contain the seeds of other ways of networking in the world.

Often, the limitations of community networks are framed in terms of their technical constraints. Wi-Fi networks are limited by the technological affordances of 2.4 GHz and 5 GHz spectrum — they use waves that by nature don't travel very far and are easily absorbed by weather and by the built environment — and by the power transmission regulations under which such networks operate: because Wi-Fi is communal, power is reduced to avoid interference. As a consequence, Wi-Fi networks favor 'line of sight' links, where wireless antennas are in view of one another. These characteristics tend to limit the scale and extent of community Wi-Fi networks. But focusing on the technical limitations of the communal spectrum risks overlooking the more troubling ideological limitations of community Wi-Fi network projects.

---

3   War-driving produced online maps, while war-chalking was a practice where open and closed nodes were marked in physical space using spray paint or chalk. War-driving continues today with websites such as WiGLE.net

4   Cory Doctorow, Paul Holman, Bruce Potter, Adam Shand, et al., 'The Wireless Commons Manifesto' (2001), https://github.com/greyscalepress/manifestos/blob/master/content/manifestos/2002-12-30-Wireless-Commons-Manifesto.txt.

5   Elinor Ostrom, *Governing the Commons: The Evolution of Institutions for Collective Action*, Cambridge: Cambridge University Press, 1990.

6   See, respectively, 'The Compact for a Free, Open & Neutral Network (FONN Compact)', https://guifi.net/en/FONNC; 'Pico Peering Agreement v1.0', http://picopeer.net/; 'Network Commons License', https://wiki.p2pfoundation.net/Network_Commons_License.

7   The best example of the latter is Rhizomatica in Oaxaca, Mexico; an open-source phone network that operates in the absence of rural cellular infrastructure. See Rhizomatica, https://www.rhizomatica.org/.

1. TECHNO-FETISHISM

At an ideological level, community network projects often conflate the specifics of their technical infrastructure with the kinds of social and economic behaviors the community network hopes to cultivate. Primavera de Filippi once argued that such technical infrastructure offered 'an internet-native model for building community and governance', for example.[8] Thus, non-hierarchical, decentralized or distributed topologies are often held to actually cultivate equally non-hierarchical forms of interpersonal cooperation within the network, while technical features such as the ability of devices to dynamically connect, and for networks to form and reconfigure without the need for a centralized intermediary, are confused with principles such as democratic decision-making and non-hierarchical social structures.

Christina Dunbar-Hester's work on cooperation in hacker, maker, and open-source radio communities shows that the opposite may be the case:[9] there are practices at work in the imagined community of the wireless commons that are strongly exclusionary on the basis of education, gender, race and class. New entrants to technical and politicized spaces often experience resistance from the existing community – there is a need, or implied demand, for one to demonstrate that one should be accepted, via displays of different forms of linguistic, technical and/or social capital.

As one example, there is a significant gender gap in digital activist communities, and in radio activism in particular. As Christina Dunbar-Hester has said of micro-radio communities, 'these practices have a long history of association with white middle-class masculinity'.[10] This goes back to the exclusively male environments of early wireless clubs, synonymous with the fantastical 'boy' inventor,[11] right up to the gender composition of mesh-networking communities today. Often, there is a denigration of women and a devaluation 'women's work' within these networked activist communities, however closely certain historically and stereotypically 'feminine' forms of cooperation and communication may resemble the very forms of cooperation that these communities hope to cultivate.[12] Issues of class and race are also sometimes overlooked in the construction of networked activist communities. Digital activism is often tied in with communities and practices that have high cultural capital.[13] Then, there is also the cost of participation: when and if community networks engage in electronic forms of civil disobedience, the consequences may be much greater for people of color than for their white counterparts.[14] Then again, there are instances when it is possible to argue

8   Primavera De Filippi, 'It's Time to Take Mesh Networks Seriously', *WIRED Magazine* (2 January 2014), https://www.wired.com/2014/01/its-time-to-take-mesh-networks-seriously-and-not-just-for-the-reasons-you-think/.

9   Christina Dunbar-Hester, *Low Power to the People: Pirates, Protest and Politics in FM Radio Activism*, Cambridge, MA: MIT Press, 2014.

10   Dunbar-Hester, *Low Power to the People*, p. 187.

11   See Douglas, *Inventing American Broadcasting*.

12   Hilary Wainwright, speaking at procomuns meetup, Barcelona, March 2016.

13   Juliet Schor, 'How to Build and Sustain Cooperative Platforms', presented at Platform Cooperativism, The New School, New York, 15-16 November 2015.

14   For example, Stephen Dunifer, white, of Free Radio Berkeley was threatened by the FCC with a significant fine for operating a pirate radio station, while Mbanna Kantako, the black instigator of a

(as Larissa Mann does, in her work on pirate-radio communities) that exclusion isn't always a bad thing:[15] in contrast to the agnostic openness of the open-source community, for example, a level of access-control can be part of what allows a group to form a coherent identity. All of which suggests that we have to let go now, if we have not done so already, of an idealized image of community networks as democratically 'open' spaces.

2. THE LIMITATIONS OF 'THE COMMONS', AS UNDERSTOOD AMONG COMMUNITY NETWORKS

Community networks may argue that radio spectrum is, and should be treated as, a 'commons', but the way this concept has been utilized doesn't challenge contemporary property relations, models of progress or the subjectivities that capitalist networks cultivate. In 2001, a number of key individuals involved with alternative wireless networks penned the Wireless Commons Manifesto, a framework for developing a global, independent, open, public network. The authors stressed the need to scale and federate localized wireless networks so that they might present as a viable alternative to dominant commercial telecommunications infrastructure, and argued that: 'the network is a finite resource which is owned and used by the public, and as such it needs to be nurtured by the public. This, by its very nature, is a commons.'[16]

As in the above quotation, the most frequent representation of the commons in wireless activism equates the notion of a spectrum commons with that of public goods such as national forests or fish stocks. This pragmatic approach to 'the commons' as a particular kind of 'resource' that is conducive to collective ownership, akin to Elinor Ostrom's definition of 'common-pool resources'[17] is quite distinct from thinking of it as a set of practices or subjectivities, as suggested by more radical theorists of 'the common' and 'commoning'.[18]

Ostrom's work on common-pool resources is instrumental in demonstrating that not all goods need to be governed through private property, and suggesting that certain goods might be best provisioned in fluid or cooperative ways. However, nowadays, in the face of the broader sharing economy, this appears as good old common sense, rather than radical economics; and, in the context of community networks, the treatment of the commons as an economic good per se fails to challenge the ownability of communications.

similar free radio station in the Bay Area, experienced intimidation, destruction of personal property and imprisonment for continuing to operate. Lorenzo Komboa Ervin, 'Attack on Black Liberation Radio', in Ron Sakolsky and Stephen Dunifer (eds) *Seizing the Airwaves: A Free Radio Handbook*, Scotland: AK Press, 1998, pp. 117-120, p. 119.

15   Larissa Mann, 'Pirate Radio: Nonlinear Innovation for Autonomous Culture', presented at Radical Networks, Berlin, 2018.

16   Doctorow et al., 'Wireless Commons Manifesto'.

17   Elinor Ostrom, *Governing the Commons: The Evolution of Institutions for Collective Action*, Cambridge: Cambridge University Press, 1990.

18   See, respectively, Michael Hardt, 'The Common in Communism', *Rethinking Marxism* 22 (3) (2010): 346-356; Peter Linebaugh, *The Magna Carta Manifesto: Liberties and Commons for All*, Berkeley: University of California Press, 2008; David Bollier, 'Commoning as a Transformative Social Paradigm', *The Next System Project* 28 (2016), https://thenextsystem.org/commoning-as-a-transformative-social-paradigm.

Furthermore, cooperation in the wireless commons often includes economic principles for incentivizing collaboration. The imagined user within the community wireless network is an economic actor who needs to be nudged in the right direction with appeals to self-interest. Ostrom goes a long way toward disproving Garret Hardin's theory of 'The Tragedy of the Commons', which argues that individuals are too self-interested to manage resources without price or state regulation.[19] In contrast, Ostrom documents many instances where communities have collectively managed goods outside of public or commercial control. Nonetheless, Ostrom's rules for governing the commons tend to focus on competitive principles for managing cooperation. In line with this argument, Pierre Dardot and Christian Laval claim that Ostrom's conception of the 'commons' supplies not only a system of rules that can be applied to the government of a shared resource, but also a set of inducements for structuring individual behavior. In this sense, they argue, Ostrom is part of the problematic of neoliberal governmentality, according to which 'the conduct of individuals can only be led by a combination of incentives and disincentives'.[20] By beginning from the assumption that users are selfish, we may inadvertently create rules that entrench those behaviors.

Just as the 2001 Wireless Commons Manifesto emphasized the need to scale beyond the locality of community networks and the propagation limitations of 2.4 GHz spectrum, the vision of the commons now held by community wireless networks is often based on a desire to build scalable alternatives to commercial or state infrastructure, something that's increasingly difficult to accomplish in the face of monolithic platforms. 'Scalability' means that the scale of a project may smoothly be changed (usually increased) without change to the project's structuring framework, and so to build, expand, and federate local relations.[21] Scalability can be a very good thing, allowing alternative, non-market forms of cooperation to expand beyond a local level and so present as reasonable alternatives. However, the concept of scalability relies on a particular vision of what success or progress looks like, and it might not be the best one. The anthropologist Anna Tsing, for example, argues that scalability, wherein 'progress' is defined in terms of the ability to expand projects without transforming their framing assumptions, is a modernist project that requires project elements to ignore the messy indeterminacies of individual encounters,[22] thus banishing, or overlooking, the kinds of meaningful diversity that might trouble or change things.

In sum, the ideology of 'the commons' that is most common among community wireless networks inadvertently reproduces many of the relations that they intend to work against. At the very least, they may be seen often to proceed from some of the same ideological assumptions that platform capitalism helps to reproduce – in this case, that: a) communication and social production are 'things' with definable boundaries that can be parceled out and managed; b) human agents are economic actors whose individual

19   Garrett Hardin, 'The Tragedy of the Commons', *Science* 162 (3859) (1968): 1243-1248, https://science. sciencemag.org/content/162/3859/1243.
20   Pierre Dardot and Christian Laval, *Commun. Essai sur la révolution au XXIe siècle*, Paris: La Découverte, 2015.
21   Anna Tsing, *The Mushroom at the End of the World: On the Possibility of Life in Capitalist Ruins*, London: Princeton University Press, 2015.
22   Tsing, *The Mushroom at the End of the World*.

behavior needs to be nudged in the right direction; c) the directive to scale and federate should take precedence over the messiness of local relations.

Finally, it's increasingly difficult to speak of the commons today, when modes of open access, sharing, and cooperativism are no longer antithetical to the functioning of capitalism. Instead, these are now the very practices that shore up the system and keep things afloat. As neoliberal economies suffer through environmental degradation and falling profit margins, forms of social production such as these are now drawn inside the market, in a move which Paolo Virno refers to as the 'communism of capital',[23] and George Caffentzis as the 'neoliberal plan B'.[24] If there was ever a moment when community Wi-Fi could be seen as diametrically opposed to commercial networks, that moment has passed. Increasingly, commercial networks see community-operated and maintained spaces as 'positive externalities' – free goods – to be exploited. One example is the now-common practice wherein commercial mobile networks offload their own congested traffic into open Wi-Fi networks.[25] The complexity of the current situation makes it much harder to speak of open networks, or resistance in these spaces, as alternative to, or outside the dominant economic system.

Imagining Alternatives

I found these issues hard to grapple with. If community networks and their alternatives are not the answer, where, and to what else, might we begin to look? Is it perhaps, rather, about asking different questions of existing network infrastructures? Instead of asking how community networks might present alternatives to commercial infrastructures and platforms, for example, could it be more fruitful now to ask what seeds of resistance and ways of commoning might be flourishing within these commercial spaces themselves? Imagining, or fictioning, offers one approach. At a Radical Networks event in New York,[26] October 2015, Rob Ray and Adam Rothstein presented a speculative narrative, entitled 'A History of the Future of Solarpunk Ham Radio Club'. Let's start with their story:

In 2016, three coastal super-storms flooded most of the West Coast of the United States, destroying all critical infrastructure. A small, previously unknown group calling themselves 'The Solarpunk Ham Radio Club' emerged to fill the communications void. Building on the detritus of a failed infrastructure, they re-established autonomous networks of communication; drying out coaxial cable, rescuing speakers and batteries from abandoned vehicles and constructing antennas from salvaged tin cans and scrap metals.

---

23   Paolo Virno, *A Grammar of the Multitude*, London: Semiotext(e), 2003.
24   George Caffentzis, 'The Future of "The Commons": Neoliberalism's "Plan B" or the Original Disaccumulation of Capital?' *New Formations* 69 (2010): 23-41.
25   Unknown Author, 'More than 60% of global mobile data traffic will be offloaded onto WiFi networks this year', *Fon.com* (Madrid, 07 April 2017), https://fon.com/pr-mobile-data-traffic-will-offloaded/.
26   Radical Networks is a series of conferences held in New York and Berlin, at which this kind of imaginative engagement with the actual and speculative possibilities of wireless activism is currently ongoing.

This was not so much about rebuilding as it was about working *within* disorientation, distress and breakdown. The new infrastructure that grew up was a 'Jugaad', built via the quick-and-dirty engineering of whatever was readily available: [27] ad hoc mesh-networks and phone systems; low-powered FM; packet-radio internet; hacked FRS and GMRS radios, and a D-star repeater controlled by a Raspberry Pi. The members established skill-shares, and taught analog radio and basic electronics. The Solarpunks couldn't duplicate the old infrastructural models, but nor did they want to. Through making-do and repurposing, they found ways of working together and learning from one another, and these practices made their networks resilient in a way that monetary investment alone could not have.

As described here, the Solarpunk Ham Radio Club is a 'degrowth' movement for amateur radio makers. 'Solarpunk ham radio' indicates a shifting away from many of the features of information capitalism, such as centralized network control and ubiquitous surveillance; it also constitutes an attempt to move past some of the common pitfalls of digital activism, and to establish a new ethics of communications infrastructure. The Solarpunk Radio story featured here reimagines relationships to communications and the materiality of networks, where connectivity relies as much on social bonds as technical architecture. The model stresses self-governed networks and peer-production, but with a focus-shift from universal service provision to individual applications and use-cases, and from macro-level infrastructures to quite local and situated innovations. There is also an emphasis on material ingenuity, in the ways the networks are designed and implemented.

I find this story useful as a blueprint for beginning to rethink commoning in community networks: not as a project that requires decentralized topologies or scale or economic incentives, but as a set of practices that can support, nourish, and innovate from subject-positions of precarity and disillusionment.

This Solarpunk-imaginary has echoes of Lizzie Borden's *Born in Flames,* a 1983 film that depicts a future pirate-radio community peopled by black and queer women who – finding that they are still marginalized in the aftermath of a social-democratic revolution that has failed to bring justice to women and minorities, and is instead backsliding into pre-revolutionary white-patriarchal structures – use wireless media to 'reformulate desire and rekindle hope'.[28] Two pirate radio stations run by women – Radio Ragazza and Phoenix Radio – come together to contest the situation by troubling mainstream representations of their post-revolutionary society. Using guerilla tactics, they take over mainstream media in order to 'redirect meaning [...] reclaim the language'.[29] Like the Ray and Rothstein's Solarpunk-imaginary, Borden's film constitutes anti-capitalist critique; the film can also be read as a critique of left-hacker culture and its promise of a universalism and equality which, in practice, threatens to betray its constituent social movements, and all of their most radical possibilities. Both the Solarpunk

---

27   Jugaad is a form of innovation, common in India, in which technical fixes are improvised using available resources. For more, see Amit S. Rai, *Jugaad Time: Ecologies of Everyday Hacking in India*, Durham, NC: Duke University Press, 2019.
28   *Born in Flames* (dir. Lizzie Borden, 1983).
29   Betty Sussler, 'Lizzie Borden by Betty Sussler', *Bomb Magazine* (October 1983), http://bombmagazine. org/article/333/lizzie-borden.

fiction above, and *Born in Flames*, model ways of using infrastructure as a mode of resistance; in both cases, a radical aesthetics is performed from a position of precarity and disequilibrium. Significantly, both of these fictions describe ways of working *through* dystopia, creating political agency in situations that may seem hopeless or beyond redemption. See also, Anna Tsing's work: 'What emerges in damaged landscapes, beyond the call of industrial promise and ruin?'.[30]

INVENTIVE MATERIAL PRACTICES

As well as being a speculative imaginary of how our networks could be otherwise, The Solarpunk Ham radio story models some of the possibilities of existent inventive material practices that run counter to network capitalism, including the hacking, repurposing and reverse-engineering practices inherent to community wireless networks, Shanzai phone culture,[31] and Indian Jugaad culture.[32]

Inventive material practices have been a part of community radio cultures from their inception.[33] In the early days of amateur radio, makers shared details of the best domestic materials with which to build radio sets, including bicycle parts, steel bed frames, and cake tins; the Quaker Oats can was a particular favorite.[34] More recently, Katrina Jungnickel's 2016 sociological study of backyard Wi-Fi technologists describes the rich material cultures of community wireless networks, involving scavenging, gleaning, signal stumbling,[35] and various ad hoc modifications to off-the-shelf electronics.[36] Today, many wireless communities around the globe hold workshops in, for example, antenna-building; maker sites detail how to home-make radio antennas and waveguides with coffee cans, electric fans, Pringles tins, and kitchenware,[37] while software radio communities are putting together powerful devices that can mimic base stations, using cheap USB television tuners sourced online.[38]

30   Tsing, *The Mushroom at the End of the World*, p. 18.
31   Roel Roscam Abbing and Dennis de Bel, *R&D: A Low-end Rich Media Publication*, Rotterdam: WORM Parallel University Press, 2014.
32   Rai, *Jugaad Time*.
33   See, for example, the work of The Critical Engineering Working Group, https://criticalengineering.org/, and the artist/engineer Surya Mattu, https://www.suryamattu.com/#/.
34   Douglas, *Inventing American Broadcasting, 1899-1922*.
35   Arguably, this attitude extends not only to hardware and software interventions in wireless networks, but also to the mapping of radio signals and network connections. 'Stumbling' is a practice wherein community network users move through a geographic area in the vicinity of their network, to see if they can locate the signal of the network and form a new network connection. If a signal can be identified, a line-of-sight base station will be installed to extend the network. The term 'stumbling' captures the embodied and imprecise nature of the practice (not unlike the opportunistic 'poking around' involved in 'circuit-bending' on the listen for new connections), which is quite different to the 'polarity calculations' of commercial engineering.
36   Katrina Jungnickel, *DIY WiFi: Re-imagining Connectivity*, London: Palgrave Macmillan, 2016.
37   See, for example, Diana Eng, 'Listening to Satellites with a Homemade Yagi Antenna', *MAKE: PROJECTS* (18 December 2012), https://makezine.com/projects/make-24/homemade-yagi-antenna/.
38   In 2013, hackers started to repurpose USB television tuners in order to reach a range of frequencies from 24 MHz to over 10000 MHz. Such tuners currently cost approximately 20 € and are readily available from Amazon and Alibaba, for example. Combined with open-source applications such as

Collated by the artist Roel Roscam Abbing, *Pretty Fly for a Wi-Fi* is an archive of wireless antennae built from everyday materials. Pots and pans, cans and plastic, discarded kitchen implements, and other trashed items are combined with careful calibration. For the project, and as a testament to a vision of alternative infrastructure, the artist built, tested, and documented these experimental designs for antennae, revisiting 'their histories, origins and uses' in the process.[39] One image shows a plastic CD-container spool, now-defunct, at the center of an antenna; others feature, respectively, a used-sardine-can antenna casing; a sieve; a wok, a plastic water-bottle, and a potato-steamer. Each object evokes an alternative internet, engaging the individuals and groups who have tried to reconfigure the dominant infrastructure to meet specific needs and desires. These inventive material practices, often falling somewhere between art-making, critical design interventions, and responses to material necessities, articulate a challenge to the business models of the platform and the commercial network, as follows:

First, these inventive practices provide a necessary antidote to the proprietary nature of network infrastructure. Two significant developments in open-source wireless networking have emerged from willfully inventive actions such as these, in which proprietary hardware devices were opened, examined, and played around with until the engineer in question could reliably reproduce their schematics. In 2004, the Catalonian engineer Ramon Roca purchased a bunch of Linksys wireless routers on a trip to California. His examination of them would become the starting point for guifi.net, the world's largest independent wireless network, running through Spain. Likewise, the open-source programmer Harald Welte's 2006 decision to reverse-engineer some base stations he purchased on eBay formed the basis for much of the open-source cellular software underpinning the Rhizomatica network.[40]

Second, the pedagogy that surrounds inventive material practices such as these itself often embodies a belief that both this knowledge, and the signals it enables to be conveyed, are themselves a kind of commons. If you attend a NETworkshop at Weise7,[41] or at Radical Networks,[42] for example; or an antenna-building BattleMesh workshop;[43] you'll see that material know-how is circulated and given away for free.

Third; making, tinkering around and taking things apart helps to make both the models and the politics of wireless systems more explicit. Sending a file over a packet-radio network, or

GQRS, broadcast signals can easily be turned into readable data. Marc DaCosta describes applications including downloading images form weather satellites as they fly overhead; tracking airplanes that fly nearby; and even using information from unintentional radio emissions to reconstruct computer interfaces. Marc Da Costa, 'How To Explore The Hidden World Of Waves All Around You', *Vice Magazine* (18 December 2017), https://www.vice.com/en_us/article/59wpmn/how-to-explore-the-hidden-world-of-radio-waves-all-around-you

39   'Pretty Fly for a Wi-Fi', http://v2.nl/archive/works/pretty-fly-for-a-wifi.
40   Andrew Back, 'Building a GSM network with open source', *The H* (26 March 2012), http://www.h-online.com/open/features/Building-a-GSM-network-with-open-source-1476745.html%3Fpage=2.
41   The Critical Engineering Working Group, NETworkshops, e.g: https://criticalengineering.org/courses/networkshop/.
42   Radical Networks, https://radicalnetworks.org/.
43   BattleMeshV12 Events, https://www.battlemesh.org/BattleMeshV12/Events.

delving into what it takes to build your own ad hoc mesh, introduces a user to the ins and outs of communication protocols. As such, this sort of 'messing around' is so much more than 'just' messing around – it's a political practice. And, while we shouldn't idealize these practices, and need also to recognize the ways in which they are often reincorporated into commercial systems, we should also recognize the spaces in which they occur as those of imaginative and materially discursive resistance to capitalist enclosure. We might go so far as to suggest that it's in these kinds of practices, rather than in manifesto-style calls for open access, that 'commoning' truly occurs.

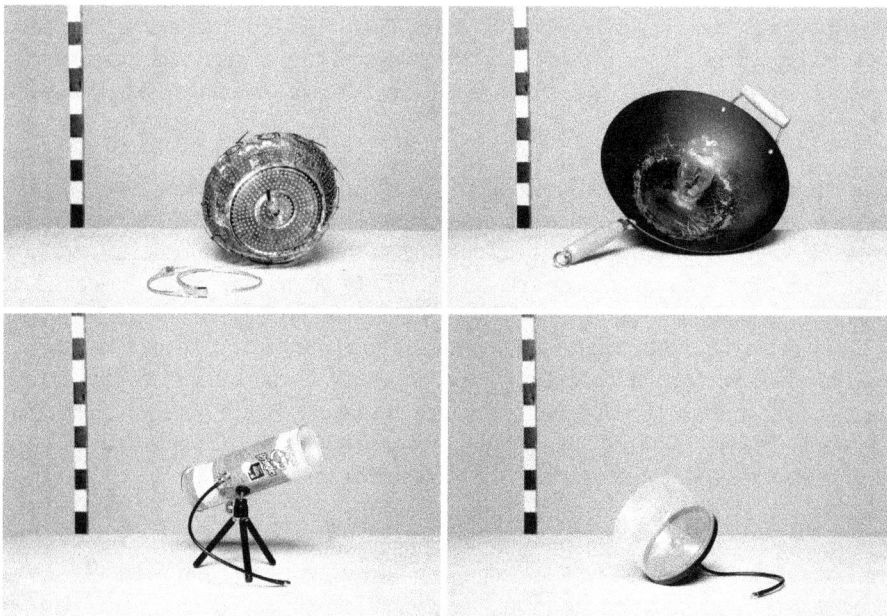

Fig. 1-4: Roel Roscam Abbing, Pretty Fly for a Wi-Fi, 2014.

LOCAL AND OFFLINE NETWORKS

One of the most intriguing aspects of the Solarpunk Ham radio imaginary is the way it abandons typical modernist ideas of progress and success when it looks to the future of community networking. These are networks where scalability and seamless global connectivity are no longer desirable end-points. Instead of viewing the often limited, often closed spaces of community wireless networks as signs of failure, could we start to think of these as blueprints for other ways of networking in the world?

In an effort to incorporate more-than-human entities into networks, the artist Tega Brain designs wireless routers to function according to particular environmental constraints, so that seamless connectivity is no longer the end goal. In the 2016 device-series *Being Radiotrophic*, Brain has created three wireless routers, devices that are normally designed to pick up broadband signals and transmit them through an urban space as effectively as possible, and made their signals contingent on haptic external elements. 'An Orbit' produces signals that wax and wane with the lunar cycle, while 'The Woods' is a hybrid house-plant/router whose connective properties are disrupted if the plant isn't watered frequently enough. 'Open Flame' associates internet connectivity with a lit candle, cutting out whenever the candle is extinguished.[44] Much like Anthony Dunne and Fiona Raby's explorations of electromagnetic connectivity and associated devices in *Hertzian Tales*, these speculative objects are material prompts to rethink connectivity.[45] In Brain's devices, wireless is not the seamless, global mesh of the 5G-imaginary. Instead, the devices probe, disrupt and cause the viewer to speculate about the kinds of contingencies and care that communications may require in future.

Larissa Mann's research concerns pirate-radio stations run by diasporic communities in Brooklyn, which, Mann suggests, are a way for marginalized communities to claim space for themselves, to build and reinforce their own communities through language and culture, and to circulate important information and resources. In contrast to the idea of radio as a boundless broadcast medium, many of these pirate stations operate within very localized geographies. And, far from offering the kind of open access that is so often extolled in certain forms of alternative media, access to participation in these stations must be negotiated. In terms of material practices (and despite the relative density of licensed radio stations in the New York area), it is notable that these communities continue to use analog broadcast technologies instead of availing themselves of internet alternatives such as online messaging, social media or digital radio technologies.[46]

Here, these community networks present with material practices that are *not* integral to the sphere of cutting-edge digital practices such as open-source, blockchain and decentralized mesh networks, but, rather, as revenants of contemporary communication technologies' past. These networks are not scalable, nor do they strive for scalability; they are neither distributed nor decentralized, but, rather, localized, finite, pragmatic; perhaps even closed; and they may be managed in agonistic ways. How do these networks allow us to think differently about the limitations of wireless media? Might we view their characteristic propagation and physical interactions with specific environments as unique strengths, rather than as limitations? Perhaps we might also re-think the roles of noise and positive disruption in our networks? Could these, in a real sense, be contributing more-than-human agencies to our networks, enabling more-than-human connectivity?

Practices such as these offer other models for the commons and the community network: models that are not governed by ideas of progress, scalability, techno-social democracy, or by game-theory models of human cooperation. Such practices may be hidden in plain sight; often they emerge from very pragmatic relationships at the margins of

44   Tega Brain, *Being Radiotropic* (2016), http://tegabrain.com/Being-Radiotropic.
45   Anthony Dunne, *Hertzian Tales: Electronic Products, Aesthetic Experience and Critical Design*, Cambridge MA: MIT Press, 2006.
46   Mann, 'Pirate Radio: Nonlinear Innovation for Autonomous Culture'.

neoliberal capitalism, from crisis and ruin and from not having enough. They are not utopian or ideal; they exemplify micro-strategies that a) work and b) embrace positions of pragmatism, of precarity; of locality rather than scalability; and of difference, agonism and even discord, rather than technologically enabled cooperation; of seamfulness and patchiness rather than seamless connectivity.

EVERYTHING WE BUILD

IN CONVERSATION:

AAY LIPAROTO AND LORENA JUAN

EVERYTHING WE BUILD

IN CONVERSATION: AAY LIPAROTO AND LORENA JUAN

Feminist queer 'spaces' are often far more than just bars, just book clubs, just dances, just sports teams, just magazines, or just performances. They are sites of community building, sites of resistance, sites of political organisation, sites of transformation, sites of healthcare, sites of survival, and sites of knowledge creation. How can we record and share these queer feminist practices in a meaningful way for our communities? What can we learn from each other?[1]

Multidisciplinary artist Aay Liparoto and their long-time co-conspirator, curator Lorena Juan met in Berlin in 2011 and soon spent their Friday nights discussing art and feminism around the kitchen table. Within the frame of Liparoto's collaborative project *Not Found On* (2019–ongoing) and audio installation *no bodies welcome | all bodies welcome* (created with HOT BODIES – CHOIR,[2] 2019), the pair share thoughts on their joint interests in community building and strategies for celebrating queer feminist knowledge both online and 'IRL'.[3]

Now based in Brussels, Aay Liparoto works with long-term performance as a form of research in order to examine the power in the banal. Liparoto's output is predominately video, text and performance, using accessible technology, personal digital archives and DIY strategies to reflect on the mechanics of the everyday life. In her curatorial practice, Lorena Juan works with experimental formats, public space, and collaborative processes. She is a cofounder of artists' collective and online platform COVEN BERLIN, which aims to create an open sphere for deconstructing assimilated social structures of sexuality and gender. Their practices and research have solidified on common ground, although their meetings are often held in cyberspace.

Lorena Juan: Over the last decades, through the democratization of digital technologies and the digitalization of society, we have seen how social movements and political art have found new forms of expression, community, and connection. Since its inception, the internet has been a transformative space for artists, especially for those belonging to groups that have been historically excluded or confined to the private sphere. Queer and feminist activism has certainly found new tools in new media. How do you see your practice and *Not Found On* in particular within this genealogy?

Aay Liparoto: As an artist I engage with deconstructing the power dynamics of everyday objects – I am a person with a body and a phone and I rarely leave the house naked. Our daily life is saturated by new and old technologies, tools that transform us and with which we coexist. Clothes and mobile phones are technologies of bodily extension that we use to code/signal to various publics. However, with phones, the scale of the public is different. I am interested

---

1   Text from *Not Found On* introduction, 2019.
2   HOT BODIES – CHOIR, Gérald Kurdian, <www.wearehotbodiesofthefuture.org>.
3   This conversation has been edited for print.

in actively using such technologies to question how their materials produce behaviours and what capacity to shift, disrupt and demystify we might have.

This questioning led me to initiate *Not Found On,* a collaborative project to create an online space to record, share, and value queer feminist arts and social knowledge. The project is based on an open source wiki structure, and has been designed, developed and written through workshops with, by, and for queer feminist bodies. Through the collective processes of thinking and making, there is an invitation to question the culture and politics of the online platforms in which we participate, the idea that 'the internet in itself offers no guarantee of transformation.'[4]

LJ: Was *Not Found On* born out of the urgency of creating an alternative to Wikipedia for queer feminist knowledge sharing?

AL: Initially I was invited to publish my book *Andrew Has His Period* within the frame of an accessible archive, which came out of my experiences of researching and struggling to gain access to media and information in remote feminist archives due to their location, high price, or being out of print. How to publish, value and share access was pivotal. It seemed natural to look at Wikipedia's recording; however I soon realised that what I was proposing would not be eligible based on their benchmarks for inclusion: a writing style with a 'neutral standpoint', no original content, required notability and criteria of verifiability.

I began applying these conditions to much of the culture, magazines, spaces, and artists, I respect, read, and visit, and it became clear that almost all of them would not be accepted, including whole communities and networks across multiple cities. These are networks of self-organized counter-publics evolved from the need to fill gaps in mainstream publishing and programming. However, in order to be included in Wikipedia, they would need the validation of mainstream media to be acknowledged as legitimate. It was a reminder of the emptiness of the statement 'the free encyclopedia that anyone can edit.'[5] – In reality, a space with rigid power structures and inherent race and gender biases, where some types of knowledge are respected and others aren't.

Where do feminist queer bodies value and share knowledge created by our communities? Facebook pages, tumblrs, reddit, email newsletters, their own websites, archives, zines, bars, kitchen tables? What are the politics of the spaces we use? Who owns the data and images collected? How are our experiences regulated and shared?

LJ: Wiki technologies have been around for quite a while. Why should we still use them?

AL: Wikis are not sexy. They are clunky, labour intensive and totally have their limitations. Still, they are an open source tool that enables co-writing among larger numbers of people and

---

4   Elisabeth J. Friedman, *Interpreting the Internet: Feminist and Queer Counterpublics in Latin America,* Berkeley: University of California Press, 2016, p. 4.

5   See Wikipedia's description on the main page, https://en.wikipedia.org/wiki/Main_Page.

includes multiple media formats: text, audio, and video. It is also stable and easy to install your own version. And, crucially, it has a large community sustaining the technology, which is necessary with a limited budget, for the longevity of the project.

There is still the simple beauty of the visible history function, transparency about the evolution of ideas through the evolving layers of an entry. I stepped into this wiki world through the project and have found it a good space to slow down, to step back from the seduction of smooth operating sites and to become more aware of organising structures. A learning and testing space, this slowness allows more time to question what and why we want to share.

In some ways the desire to create a space to document 'queerness', something sticky and blurry, something essentially undefined within a wiki is absurd. The *Not Found On* wiki desires to be more of a junction box, collecting certain pieces of knowledge while also connecting out to other sites, projects and networks.

LJ: There is something inherently queer about collective work in the arts, about defying the idea of the autonomy of the single author. Is meeting in real life for collaborative co-writing sessions a big part of *Not Found On*?

AL: Meeting and working together is so vital in order to understand our relationships to each other via digital technologies. Co-learning and co-creating is essential to *Not Found On* as a feminist practice. The project launched in March 2019 with a think-tank day with ten guests who work around queer DIY publishing, activism and organising, such as yourself (Lorena Juan), Mert Sen, Tyna Adebowale, Marnie Slater and Karol Radziszewski. The aim was to discuss how to create a safer online space for recording and sharing queer knowledge. There was also a workshop by Just For The Record, a group that addresses 'how gender is represented in new media and writing/publishing tools like Wikipedia, and what influence this has on the way history is recorded'.[6] The event, hosted at WORM Rotterdam to coincide with International Women's Day, was really a catalyst point to flag concerns and for proposing strategies.

The project has been built through existing networks of DIY queer feminist organisations over eleven subsequent workshops in Brussels, Liverpool and Rotterdam. The site went live in May 2019 and has been shaped by around ninety-five queer feminists, in particular social designer Cristina Cochior and in various capacities, Laura Deschepper, Priya Sharma, Carlos Marfil Rodriguez and Conway. *Not Found On* is an intensive on-going process of co-learning, with everything built step by-step via IRL workshops. Our most pressing focus is working with different groups to test and adapt the input forms, interfaces, and design accessibility.

There is an intense labour in collective work that requires time and care and also allows for error and accountability. The desire to have a physical community is something that has come up over and over again in our workshops, and will remain at the project's heart. We are still seeking collaborators to work with us in defining the space further.

6   Just for the Record, http://justfortherecord.space/.

LJ: Is your work with HOT BODIES – CHOIR an extension of this practice?

AL: *no bodies welcome | all bodies welcome* made in collaboration with HOT BODIES – CHOIR, is about the embodied experience of knowledge and its transmission. The desire was to create a piece around this research and methodology without directly exposing the *Not Found On* platform, which has a specific public and intention.

Through a series of workshops we looked for a way to combine the writing and singing practices of HOT BODIES – CHOIR in Brussels with the co-writing of *Not Found On*. To find words and voice to together acknowledge our interdependence with digital technology as queer feminist bodies for information, work, sex, entrainment, communication, social life, healthcare and combinations of them all. In *no bodies welcome | all bodies welcome* we transmit a sticky mixture of reflections on cyberspace and offer unsolicited advice sent directly into your ear canals via an audio installation.

LJ: Virtual space can change the habits of the subjects who inhabit it and subsequently have an impact on the broader dynamics of social production and reproduction. However, as Rosi Braidotti points out, in times of great technological developments, Western society reaffirms its traditional habits, especially the tendency to create hierarchies. In what we know as 'pink washing', corporations appropriate the struggles of queer bodies in order to obtain economic and social benefits. Which strategies do you use in *Not Found On* to challenge this commodification?

AL: There are a couple of aspects I want to touch on here: first, the practical function and structure of the project *Not Found On*, and second, the reliance of marginalized bodies on commercial spaces and the idea of 'identities' going mainstream.

The project comes out of a resistance to the neatly packaged commodification of identities. It seeks to be a hub for recording a multiplicity of voices in their own complexity and connecting to other projects and people. On a practical level, we know what our server looks like, where it is located and the people/politics that care for it. This allows us to collectively run a community space, where we are able to establish our practices, code of conduct, and content. The site itself encourages tactics of obfuscation and won't sell your data.

From reddit groups on trans healthcare and queer city-based Facebook groups to specific dating apps, there is now, as ever, a great need for marginalized people to form counter-publics; to connect online and IRL to people like us and seek the information we don't find in other spaces. But what does it mean to use these often 'free' spaces that monetize our data? Friedman puts it well: 'corporations seeking to commodify user information have enclosed the so-called "internet commons" by offering a devil's bargain trading access to global networks for individual privacy.'[7] We are allowing 'our identities' to be sanitized, sold back to us at best, and exposing ourselves to real world harm, at worst. Are we suffering from digital apathy or does the need to connect to others just outweigh the time and energy required to question these spaces?

---

7   Friedman, *Interpreting the Internet*, p. 13.

I am cautious that, along with a greater presence of intersectional feminist, queer and LGBTIA+ narratives in mainstream media, there has been a rise in far-right politics across Europe and the USA and, worryingly, an increase of hate crimes. Although one might think that more visibility is a kin to breaking these power imbalances I ask: Who is telling these narratives? Who is profiting from them? I am cynical of feminism, decolonization, and queerness being 'trends'. These are not and never have been trends: they are urgencies, and as long as these systems of oppression go on, there is a need to self-organise opposition and find ways to build energy in our communities.

LJ: In questioning the spaces that we inhabit, the artwork of Tabita Rezaire comes to mind. In *Afro Cyber Resistance* (2014), she draws upon discourses of e-colonialism to show up the internet as a 'white space'. How do you see *Not Found On* in relationship to this?

AL: What resonates in Tabita Rezaire's work is the need for people to register their own knowledge and embodied experience, such as in her example of Wiki Africa, to resist being subjugated by the existing power structures, now reproduced online. The work is a call to consciousness and action.

Not Found On can't and does not seek to be applied as a one-size-fits all model. This platform comes out of the needs and desires of a particular context: created in English, in Western Europe, and tied to ideas of Western feminism, queerness, gender and LGBTIA+ narratives. We acknowledge the rich and varying articulations of gender and sexuality that exist globally and the lasting legacies of colonial laws still enacted upon predominantly black and brown queer bodies.

In its conception, *Not Found On* suggests two significations: Firstly, all that is not adequately recorded nor respected by historical and mainstream canons. The narratives we were never told in schools, the artists, thinkers, and achievements that were and are left out on the basis of class, race, religion, gender and sexuality. Secondly, the attempt of this space to house and connect diverse queer feminist experiences, while ultimately knowing that it can never and should not try to represent all.

Not Found On takes Flavia Dzodan's scream 'MY FEMINISM WILL BE INTERSECTIONAL OR IT WILL BE BULLSHIT!' as a founding statement. These lines are just lip service unless participation, action, and critique are applied. We seek to manipulate the tools and language of the site in an attempt to not submit to established power dynamics for example by looking for alternative ways to organise and search information, by embracing non-standardised language, by asking users to offer a 'politics of location'[8] statement, and by clearly stating our limitations, where the project comes from and how we are funded. The site itself invites you to be critical of the spaces you participate including ours.

---

8   Adrienne Rich, 'Notes Toward a Politics of Location (1984)', in *Blood, Bread, and Poetry: Selected Prose 1979-1985*, New York: W.W. Norton & Company, 1986, pp. 210-231.

LJ: Radical queer and feminist offline spaces employ strategies to create 'safe spaces'. Can a virtual platform aspire to be a 'safe space'? If so, which protocols should be followed?

AL: I feel that the question should always be: What is a safe space and for whom? Regardless of whether off- or online, we can only ever speak of a 'safer space' and never a 'safe space'. Safer space is more about the community and culture you build around a space which is an active and on-going process.

Our aim is to be at use for a specific public, but this of course is tricky online where there can be no expectation of privacy. We prefer not to appear in search engines, we ask not to be crawled and from our community we ask not to be shared on social media. However, this is no guarantee. It is crucial for us to make our community aware of the structure we are participating in. For example, we make it clear that you can register for an account without providing an email address or legal name. Despite this, your IP address leaves a trace and you may be identified by your location or name on an internet contract.

We do not use categories in our data structure but define each entry via an array of descriptors, some based on more literal properties such as location or form; others on energy, mood and associations. We are looking for alternative overlapping and subjective ways to find and think about content and context. We are attempting to use the wiki structure unconventionally to escape the toxicity that has been enacted via taxonomy.

Currently we are small-scale by design, and opening up to people personally via workshops. As the space grows there will be new urgencies, with the tension between protection from vandalism and reaching a wider audience. We will soon host *Not Found On* workshops looking at existing social technical protocols among feminist and LGBTQIA+ forums, private groups and archives. Seeking to collectively address whether they deter people with a legitimate claim to the space, asking how we can build community on *Not Found On* whilst addressing privacy needs.

LJ: For me *Not Found On* is about self-preservation and, at the same time, embracing vulnerability. So it may not be so far away from our initial encounters at the kitchen table and the desire to find community.

AL: It so often starts in a kitchen, I think this might be the least respected seat of knowledge but such a vital setting, especially for othered bodies! The desire to self-organise and curate the spaces we need is still so relevant, much as you do with COVEN BERLIN. While we want to develop direct community in our local areas with people we know, I think it also goes beyond connection as a purely social function — it's about supportive networks of knowledge.

I believe collective recording is key to breaking the cycle of the vibrant energies of people in the now only being 'discovered' and celebrated 20 or 30 years later when they are no longer a threat to systems in power. This silencing through lack of record in the public domain makes it much harder for that knowledge to accumulate intergenerationally.

Not Found On is one gesture towards changing that. We want to invite queer feminist bodies to join us, to take time to grow and to be allowed to fail.

'Everything you own you've had to build on stolen ground but now we build inwards. Deeper away from all pick up the stones and build with us.'[9]

---

9   Text from *Not Found On* co-writing session with 9 bodies, Liverpool, 2019.

MOLECULAR SEX AND POLYMORPHIC SENSIBILITIES

Johanna Bruckner

MOLECULAR SEX AND POLYMORPHIC SENSIBILITIES

JOHANNA BRUCKNER

Paleontologists would perhaps understand the present time as the outcome of a failed experiment with sex.[1] This text presents a number of propositions as to how recent conceptions of the molecularization of the body might crystallize in a redistribution of the sensible. The mobility of pleasure and knowledge as capital, the expansion of global supply chains, logistical computing, planetary sharing economies, and transformations in ecological systems all have implications for human relations within the world's political configurations. These new economic and social orders have largely benefited from advances in molecular research, hormonal and libidinal biology, virology, and sex/design. They enhance the human body, the molecular body, and employ it as biochemical and geopolitical material. Algorithms increasingly penetrate the micro- and nanostructures of our physical, artificial, and sexual bodies, to provide data sets for further economic and political applications. For example, biological material is used to explore the genetic engineering of sex and citizenship. Gene discovery software and research allow biological materials to be encoded, forming a basis for the invention of new physical and artificial bodies, and notions of how their sexualities might perform. The imagination of sex is one of sex/design. Furthermore, nanotechnologies and artificial intelligence shape the human experience of pleasure through technical and biomedical interventions, such as robots acting as erotic partners, or through pharmaceutical experimentation, where feeling is converted into a techno-sensory product. Biological substance, then, is translated into fluid networks of information, opening up new spheres of intellectual and molecular property. The chemical industries have situated the desires of bodies within an ensemble of social relations, in which the libidinal economy serves the sex/design of biocapitalism. In the 'pharmacopornographic era', capitalism, pornography, and the pharmaceutical industry merge to form a control society that infiltrates, penetrates, and mutates, engineering our desires from the level of hormones to pervasive media images and risk technology.[2] In contemporary aesthetic economies, pleasure is increasingly experienced as a fragile and virtual realm. Given this techno-sensual modification of human feeling, the body is continuously subjected to speculative alteration.

How might these scenarios, in which the body is thrown into a chaotic and unpredictable molecular world, enact particular situations of molecular revolutionary potential, situations that might allow for the reordering of contemporary sex/design regimes to make way for a micropolitics of the sensible? Which affectively diffracted temporalities are needed for bodies to align beyond the boundaries of representation? Within which bodily conceptions can sensual and energetic forces coexist in interrelation? Research into the molecularization

1   Eben Kirksey, 'Queer Love, Gender Bending Bacteria, and Life after the Anthropocene', *Theory, Culture, and Society* (June 3, 2018): 197-219, p. 205.
2   Paul Preciado, *Testo Junkie: Sex, Drugs, and Biopolitics in the Pharmacopornographic Era*, New York: The Feminist Press at CUNY, 2013, p. 1.

of human and artificial existence clearly becomes a matter of ethical and political concern. Advances in molecular research offer a framework for recalibrating our entangled relations with the sensible world around us. Through the perpetual bending of and movement among and between human, animal, technology, sex, and atmosphere, the molecular shapes a world beyond the tangible. It pushes at the limits of the human sensorium and invents technological prostheses that now have the capacity to disorganize, reconfigure, and redistribute sensible relations and the patterns with which subjects comprehend the world.

I.

To begin I will briefly reflect on the molecular from a labor perspective, since in the dialectic between accumulation and destitution, the molecular constitutes specific autonomies, which I will later consider in greater detail in light of Karen Barad's work. In the final third of the 20th century, work moved away from the Fordist ethos of production and toward global networks of information and finance and the realms of desire. The subsequent economic reorganization of work valued the intellectual, cognitive worker through the semiotic production of meaning, and the workplace became flexible, no longer confined to the factory. Stimulated by the dissolution of labor, life and leisure, neoliberal victories over aesthetic value led to the valorization of desire as semiotics. Today's post-Fordist regimes of cognitive labor depend on technologies as machines of desire, producing affective experiences as systems of labor.[3] Considering these machines of desire in their molecular operational processes – as a 'microphysics of the unconscious'[4] – they seem to exist as affective molecular aggregates. Dependent on their cognitive laborer, their viral host, they stimulate the constitution of social formations and abstract connectivities. So, if we view the process of affection/being affected by technology not as an appropriative strategy but rather as a metamorphic virus, the machine, as well as our relationship to it, may be a catalyzing motor to break away from capital's extraction and exploitation of our desires through affect's potential indeterminacy.

II.

Against this background of the transformation of the world via molecular bodies and their intimacies, my video installation *Molecular Sex* (2020) proposes a sex robot aimed at liberating normative technology-led worldviews of intimate relations. I chose to feature a sexbot because of the uncanny parallels between modalities of queerness and the performance of plastic. I am interested in the links between sex, plastic, and non-reproduction. Objects of sexual pleasure are chemically linked to the very plastics that, in their molecular texture, make sexual indifferences possible. Plastics carry their queerness into sex, inhibiting sexual reproduction. Sexual difference may not even turn out to have a future, as plastic mirrors a form of becoming based on technological and bacterial merging, rather than the reproductive ability of organic

---

3   I understand machines both as the technological framework that surrounds us, and in response to Félix Guattari's 'Systems of Semiotic Relations', in *Molecular Revolution, Psychiatry and Politics*, London: Penguin, 1984.
4   Félix Guattari and Gilles Deleuze, *Anti-Oedipus*, Minnesota: University of Minnesota Press, 1984, p. 200.

creatures.[5] Plastic is actualizing a queer techno-bacterial future, since the texture of plastic functions according to the logic of dispersion and polymorphic accumulation. It is less a substance than the antithesis of a substance; a paradigm in which substance is transformed into a way of being without stable presence or meaning.[6]

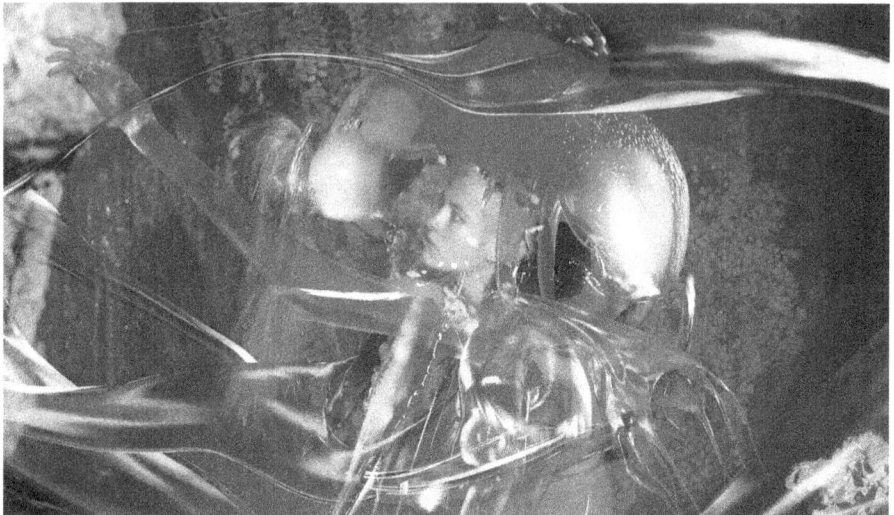

Fig. 1: Molecular Sex (still), Johanna Bruckner, 2020. 4K Video.

The sexbot's plastics are composed of an array of chemicals, produced in precarious multi-layered processes, primarily in China. In addition to the molecules referred to as plastic, plasticizers are added for pliability, color, or heat resistance. Perhaps the most infamous of these is bisphenol A (BPA), one of a number of chemicals notorious for their reproductive toxicity. BPA blocks the human ability to reproduce through both an overexposure to the hormone estrogen and by way of endocrine disruptors that mimic hormones in the body and interfere with their functions. This sometimes has the effect of queering the gender of the body it has penetrated. Such chemicals are generally imperceptible but can have drastic effects on our, and other species', bodies. Moreover, microplastics – multitudinous species that are slowly but irreversibly changing the environment – hold up a mirror to the world. These complex bacterial meshworks infiltrate synthetic surfaces, reproducing and destroying each other, mutating and developing into new organisms dependent on the sources of energy unlocked by carbon. The reproductive systems of many creatures allow them to change sex or reproduce by cellular division. Queer new worlds are inadvertently being birthed from the human quest for alien, synthetic pleasures.[7]

5   Claire Colebrook, 'Sexual Indifference', in Tom Cohen (ed) *Telemorphosis: Theory in the Era of Climate Change*, vol. 1, Ann Arbor: MPublishing/Open Humanities Press, 2012, pp. 167-182, p. 177.
6   Heather Davis, 'Imperceptibility and Accumulation: Political Strategies of Plastic', *Camera Obscura 92*, 32.2 (2016): 186-193, p. 188.
7   Davis, 'Imperceptibility and Accumulation'.

The sexbot in *Molecular Sex* acts as a prosthesis for the disconnecting and reconnecting body parts that circulate systemically in the virtual world. It dissolves into the atmospheres that surround it, using these body parts to inhale and exhale and to perform as various entities during the video. During the work, the robot learns its existence as a technoid 'trans/material' and 'tranimal' being,[8] and in so doing transforms existing principles of pleasure. First, it performs both as and with a brittle star, a deep-sea brainless animal whose body is a metamorphosing optical and sensual system. Second, it performs both as and as a host of the Wolbachia bacterium, which distorts lovemaking and sex, its bodily fluids accumulating into something like smart bombs for aleatory speciation. Third, it interacts with intersex persons, since molecular gene research has discovered that the future of sex determination involves an array of sexual variations and practices rather than a binary structure. The sexbot's plastic figurations create penetrable entities that are imperceptibly but irreversibly changing our environment.

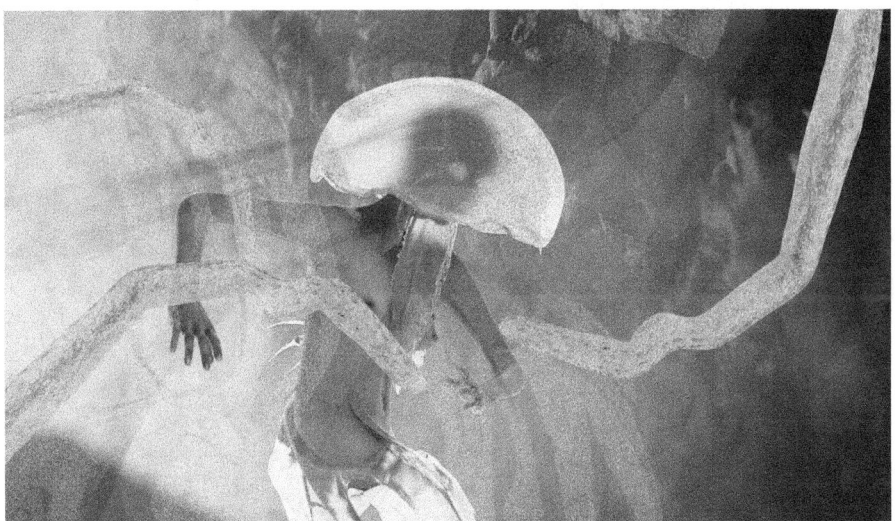

Fig. 2: Molecular Sex (still), Johanna Bruckner, 2020. 4K Video.

Let's give these three scenarios more detailed consideration. In one scenario, the sexbot acts as a brittle star. Multi-limbed and star-shaped, this living, breathing and mutating deep-sea animal offers us an opportunity to rethink normative relationships and connectivities. The brittle star is a body whose morphology, namely its intertwined skeletal and diffuse nervous systems, constitutes a system for visualization, since its epidermis consists entirely of microlenses. As an animal without a brain, being and knowing, materiality and intelligibility, substance and form collapse into one another. When at risk of capture, a brittle star breaks off the threatened body part and then regrows it. During this process, it regenerates and autonomizes its optics and other sensualities, continually reworking its geometry, topology,

8   Kirksey, 'Queer Love', pp. 6f., quoting Kelley and Hayward, 'Carnal Light: Following the White Rabbit', *parallax* 19.1 (2010): 114-127.

and bodily boundaries. Its corporeality, materially enacted, is not a matter of being specifically situated *in* the world, but rather of being *of* the world in all its dynamic specificity.[9]

Likewise, brittle star species exhibit great diversity in sexual behavior and reproduction, be this broadcast spawning or sexual dimorphism, to take just two examples. Some are hermaphroditic and self-fertilizing, while others reproduce asexually by regenerating or cloning themselves from fragmented body parts.[10]

Brittle stars are living nanotechnology. Their technical and sensual morphology, which allows them to respire and to repair themselves, is now being used as a blueprint for enterprises such as new software and computing operations, and designs in the fields of logistics and life sciences, as well as telecommunications, optical networks, and artificial pleasure machines aimed at chemosensory experience.[11] The question now is not only how these queer, nonhuman animals can be appropriated for political human and technical interests, which give shape to life-forms of unknown, aleatory orientations, but also how our desires are being co-constitutively reconfigured. In the video, the sexbot's intimacies are computed as diffraction patterns. But beyond potential computer software applications, our attunement to brittle star intra-action matters most in queering our understanding of and participation in networked realities and technological transformation, moving toward entangled forms of intra-participation.

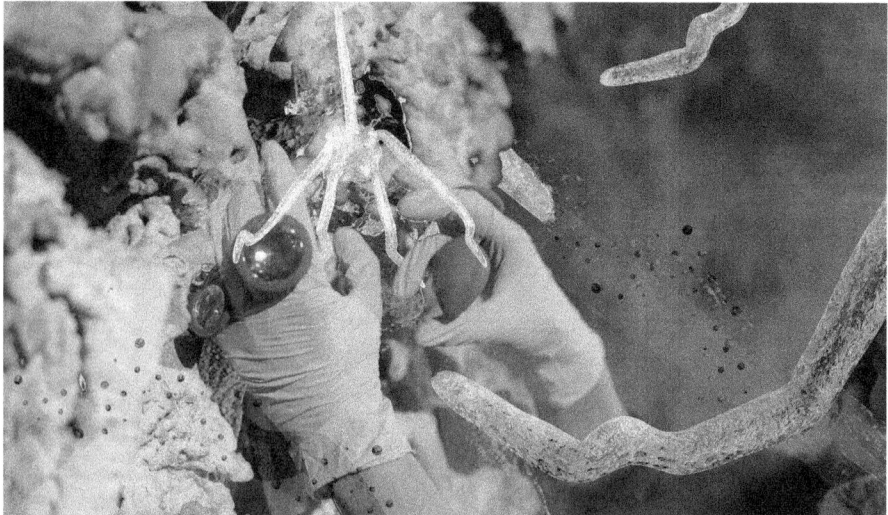

Fig. 3: Molecular Sex (still), Johanna Bruckner, 2020. 4K Video.

---

9   Karen Barad, 'Invertebrate Visions: Diffractions of the Brittlestar', in Eben Kirksey (ed) *The Multispecies Salon*, Durham: Duke University Press, 2014, pp. 221-236.
10   Barad, 'Invertebrate Visions'.
11   Barad, 'Invertebrate Visions'.

In the other scenario, the bot performs as and in relation to the Wolbachia bacterium. These hardy bacteria exist and make love in ways that are not to be disrupted by climate change or even nuclear war. Love among Wolbachia bacteria often develops in the form of temporary alliances and symbiotic attachments, connections that establish themselves like a rhizome between the different target bodies of various species, regardless of their sex. Wolbachia's queer kinship practices evolve by becoming molecular in swarms of multiplicities, with elements of the bodies crossing over into and transgressing others. Wolbachia trade genes with different species, blurring the boundaries between self and other. They sterilize the unsuspecting sexual partners of their invertebrate hosts to bring about reproductive isolation and the conditions for new speciation. They can perform gender-bending practices in host bodies, for example transforming genetic males into reproductively viable females by altering the sperm cytoplasm, that is to say the material semiotic fluid within the cell. The sperm of males infected with Wolbachia become weaponized, turning into what I previously referred to as a 'smart bomb'. To affirm the conditions of speciation, these sperm destroy the eggs of uninfected females, moving toward new cross-species of aleatory sexual entities. As micro-biopolitical agents, these bacteria disorganize the bodies of their hosts on a molecular level. Within this context, biomedical initiatives have reinforced biopolitical strategies, exploring potential human/microbe collaborations for future technological concerns in the field of social and economic equalities.[12]

In a further scenario, the emerging sexbotic figurations in the video interact with an intersex person. Instead of simple sex chromosome data — usually XX or XY — in the future there would be dozens of sex-related genes. Molecular genetics is therefore likely to require a shift from binary sex to quantum sex, with a dozen or more genes each conferring a small probability of male or female sex; their further emergence and design would depend on micro- and macro-environmental interactions. The forms of sexes and sexualities that might emerge from this quantum cloud of biological and environmental progress are still speculative.[13]

12   Kirksey, 'Queer Love', pp. 4ff.; Donna Haraway, *Staying with the Trouble: Making Kin in the Chthulucene*, Durham: Duke University Press, 2016, p. 101.
13   Vernon A. Rosario, *Quantum Sex: Intersex and the Molecular Deconstruction of Sex*, Durham: Duke University Press, 2009.

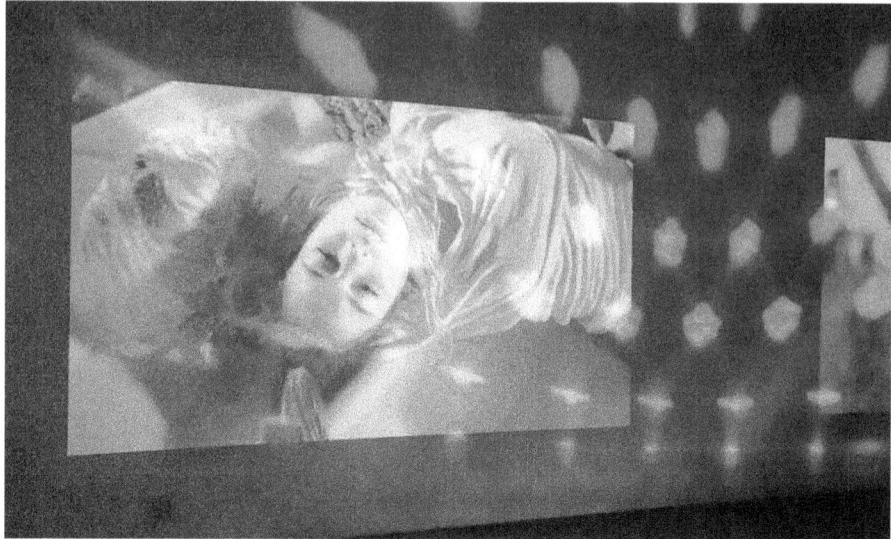

Fig. 4: Quantum Polymorphic Sensibilities. Johanna Bruckner, 2019. Installation view. Photo: Astrid Piethan.

III.

In order to better understand the corporeality of technology, matter, and desire that underpin this text, let me briefly consider Karen Barad's examinations of quantum field theory. Barad describes the inseparability of the world and object as 'intra-action', and conceives of reality as a continuum of intra-acting quantum entanglements.[14] She proposes that matter is 'characterized by self-touch – by the interaction of the particle with the surrounding electromagnetic field or virtual particles, which it itself generates and destroys – and in which it "comes into contact with the infinite alterity that it itself is."'[15] Touching and experiencing are thus regarded as the essence of what constitutes matter. This concept of matter always includes alterities – the virtual, the unpredictable – and requires 'recognition of our responsibility towards the infinity of the other.'[16] In this regard, the sensible is in continuous intra-action with itself and, as such, queers, disorders, and preempts affections and the affective machine. This understanding of the indeterminacy of the machine and the self as multiplicity is for Barad a 'superposition – an intensification of matter beyond an ordering regime.' In order to understand matter's micro-agencies, Barad introduces the concept of 'agential separability'.[17] Materials differentiate in conjunction with affective forces,

---

14   Karen Barad, 'Quantum Entanglements and Hauntological Relations of Inheritance: Dis/continuities, SpaceTime Enfoldings, and Justice-to-Come', *Derrida Today* 3.2, 2010: 240-268, p. 246ff.; Haraway, *Simians, Cyborgs, and Women.*

15   Karen Barad, 'Berühren – das Nicht-Menschliche, das ich also bin (V.1.1)', in Kerstin Stakemeier and Susanne Witzgall (eds) *Macht des Materials – Politik der Materialität*, Berlin: diaphanes, 2014, pp. 163-176. Translation by author.

16   Barad, 'Berühren'.

17   Barad, 'Berühren'.

maintaining the object-human relation in a process of perpetual diffraction and refraction. Agential separability, the agentially enacted material condition of phenomena, is what shapes and reshapes matter from within. In any given situation, there are micro-agencies on the tiniest of scales within the object-human relation, which, when intensified on a larger scale, lead to micro-revolutionary crystallizations.[18] Following Barad, we could consider these radical molecular crystallizations happening among particles of matter on a molecular level as 'phenomena [that] are not located in space or time, but are material entanglements enfolded and threaded through the spacetimemattering of the universe.'[19] Plastics do not biodegrade; they break apart, becoming smaller and smaller but remaining integral to themselves while affecting the world. These agential cuts, the micro-revolutionary formations, enact the possibilities of situational responses, which indeed produce the capability for responsibilities in each individual constellation of particles. A micro-revolutionary practice thus presupposes plural acts of becoming responsible/response-abilities. Matter, or to be more precise, our relation to our affective machines and substances, crystallizes a 'densification of the ability to react, to respond.'[20]

In more general terms, bodies and their social relations are structured by pre-symbolic or nonhuman forces – forces that are constructed as competing micro-agencies. These subjects are bodies of multiplicities, as they are diffracted across space, time, and realities. Their embodiment is their situational embedment in the environment as well as their interaction with it, as an embodied cognition.

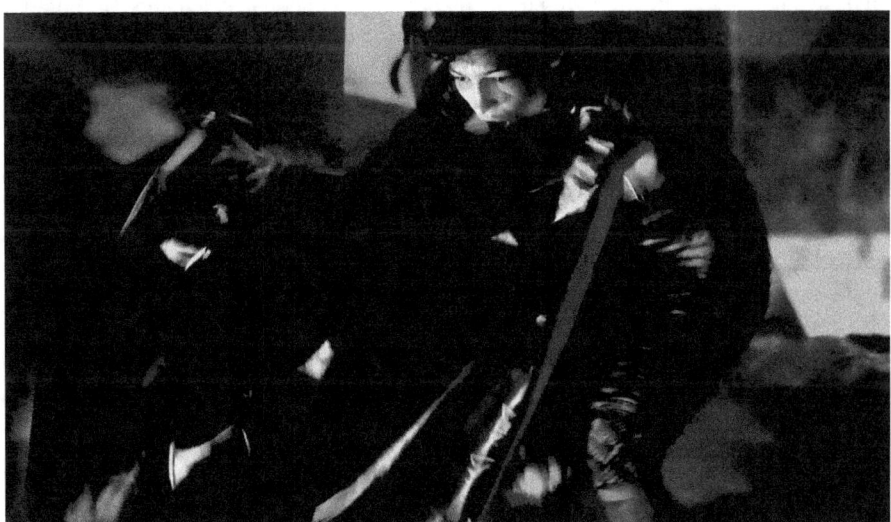

Fig. 5: *Quantum Polymorphic Sensibilities, Johanna Bruckner, 2019. Performance. Photo: Guillermo Heinze.*

18   Guattari, *Molecular Revolution*, p. 9.
19   Karen Barad, 'Quantum Entanglements and Hauntological Relations of Inheritance', p. 261.
20   Barad, 'Berühren', p. 170. Translation by author.

The installation considers the possibility of a futurity in which becoming one with animals and techno-objects is a collective participation in preternatural agency. Today's sensate technoid body — a body in which the boundaries between human and machine are always already displaced, and which includes sexbots and their artificial intelligences — can be perceived as 'a matter of material imploded entities, a body as dense material semiotic things; in between and not able to locate.'[21] However, the point of this cyborg doll then is not to blur the boundaries between human and nonhuman, but rather to understand the materializing effects of particular ways of drawing boundaries between 'humans' and 'non-humans'.[22] Their state of indeterminacy is inherent to the formation of new temporalities and spheres of desire, in which new subjects of entanglement come into being.

IV.

Even if the molecular is exploited as raw material, it may yet be an available resource for resistance. The brittle star, Wolbachia, and the plastification of the world provide examples in which the revolutionary immediacy of molecular agency can be observed as intrinsic to the non/human domain of cells and bodies. From observations of cellular behavior, a cell's metabolic networks, meshworks, and protein folding seem to be speculative materially enacted processes, since they do not exist beyond their relation to matter, which is, for Barad, an aleatory, agential process. What is more, the regime of financial valorization through biosecurity is in an unstable state of affairs, as it is almost impossible to invent an unspecifiable futurity within the molecular realm of economic calculation. In Barad's approaches to matter's capacity for intrinsic micro-agencies, the virtual is incalculable. Rather, the multitude of molecular bodily materials, as sensible relationalities, provide space for the proliferation of alternative body knowledge, for the emergence of new demands for state and corporate bodies, through the collectivization of semiotic-sensible minds. As for today's cognitive workers, the biological self is a precariously bare entity. Of central importance are the sub-ontological zones, in which confrontation and struggle take place outside the field of the recognizable and so beyond representation itself. For example, practices of alignment via molecular processes of undercommoning posit the world as yet to come, with the present held as an open field for political engagement.[23] This molecular territorialization can now refer not just to chemical and genetic processes but also to human bodies, political groupings, and assemblages: 'molecules territorialize and deterritorialize by creating ever-new groupings and then branch off into other possibilities' of human, social, and abstract connectivities.[24] The molecular temporalities that emerge, speculatively considered, generate a discontinuous history and present of their own.[25] Matter's ongoing constitution of the sensible as a series

---

21   Donna Haraway, 'Awash in Urine: DES and Premarin in Multispecies Response-ability', in *Staying with the Trouble*, pp. 104-110.

22   Karen Barad, 'Nature's Queer Performativity', in *Kvinder Køn & Forskning,* 2012, pp. 25-53, p. 31.

23   My use of 'undercommoning' comes after Stefano Harney and Fred Moten's *The Undercommons. Fugitive Planning and Black Study*, New York: Autonomedia, 2013.

24   Gilles Deleuze and Félix Guattari, *A Thousand Plateaus*, Minneapolis: University of Minnesota Press, 1987; Jordana Rosenberg, 'The Molecularization of Sexuality: On Some Primitivisms of the Present', *Theory & Event* 17.2 (2014), https://www.muse.jhu.edu/article/546470.

25   Rosenberg, 'The Molecularization of Sexuality'.

of molecular, intra-active patterns represents queer ecologies because, in their inherently resistant nature and through their aleatory figuration, the molecular becomes an abstraction. These molecules of desire become the occasion for polymorphic anticipation and embodied micro-agencies of the sensible. This process of disaffected labor, through which molecules create, cut, separate, and re-entangle their agencies, is itself an assemblage of micro-revolutionary crystallization, whose intensifications conceive of techno-human bodies as complex 'particles of possibility'.[26] Our technological machines constitute us in relation to the matter that surrounds us. The politics of desire essentially concern these assemblages of 'particles of possibility' constituted by abstract machines.[27]

V.

To conclude, the sexbot proposed in my work aims to bring to the surface the underlying micro-agencies that are enhanced in the techno-affective machinic relationship between body, desire, and matter and which constitute the multitude of precarious bodies whose 'molecular joy' represents the raw material of intimate-cognitive capitalism. In doing so, this work proposes that we urgently refine our cyborg politics, taking 'pleasure in the confusion of boundaries' and making arguments 'for responsibility in their construction.'[28]

The integration of artificial intelligence into sexbots stores information in the bot's body, through which it learns to perform as an aleatory, molecular intra-participatory sexual species. This code and the bot's subsequent actions are based on training, which makes modifications in intra-action with its environment. This training is based on data sets, which intra-actively generate data-scapes of pleasure, and which are again linked to and placed within the existing infrastructures of computing, while also redefining access and connection within computing. Rather than encouraging data's permanence, these emerging intra-active data-scapes promote polygamy, polymorphism, and randomness. The code opens up networks of as-yet unknown sensual, affective knowledge: an eternal nexus of feedback within the sym-poetic entanglement between body, sex, and technology, toward a polyrhythmic cyberspace. As a micropolitical virus, the physical and artificial body infiltrate the configuration and performance of other technical machines and their relations. Its agency should be recognized not only by its appearance as virtual pleasure, but by its ability to redistribute and contest the processes of transmission, streaming, downloading, storage, sharing, and consumption.

My starting principle for this work was the notion that the conceptions of bodies and realities proposed by artificial intelligence and such new technologies are deeply rooted in heteronormative, racist, colonial worldviews: we need to unsettle the determination of, access to, and our participation in these scenarios. Humanity must actively intervene in the disorder of biological life on all scales, in order to produce temporalities of collectively desired entanglement. What might be learned from plastics in creating political resiliency in the face of accelerating forms of biological, climatic, geologic, social, and technological

26   Guattari, *Molecular Revolution*, p. 5.
27   Guattari, *Molecular Revolution*.
28   Haraway, *Simians, Cyborgs, and Women*; Kirksey, 'Queer Love', p. 18.

change, death, and disparity? As a result of their molecular base in oil, plastics accumulate toxic potency as they move through the world and our molecular bodies.[29] It seems to me that humanity's most pressing requirement is a political order that corresponds to the corporeal techno-scientific practices; one that is not constrained by law, property, and nation, but is open to an ethical play beyond the current appropriation of life into the geopolitical biological apparatus. In maintaining refuges and spaces for undisciplined, wild, and unruly forms of life and knowledge, homes for inverts and techno-queer microbes and life-forms should be included too.[30] We need to be prepared to accept unlikely allies, recognizing that our struggles are mutual, or at least directed against common enemies: the increasing liberation of markets, austerity measures, and extractivism. The ethics of the present essentially involve finding strategies for living with toxicity, indeed accepting it as a queer future; ways of navigating horror while resisting the policies, governments, and corporations blocking new and alien life-forms from emerging.[31] In fact, no economy of technology-led transformations in polymorphic desires, sex-related affinities, and reproductive labor yet exists. The onus is on us to create systems in which future libidinal orders can find a place to affirm non/human networks as undercommoning affinities and joint temporalities.

29   Davis, 'Imperceptibility and Accumulation', p. 189.
30   Kirksey, 'Queer Love', p. 18.
31   Davis, 'Imperceptibility and Accumulation', p. 191.

ENDINGS AND NEW BECOMINGS

REQUIEM FOR THE NETWORK

GEERT LOVINK

REQUIEM FOR THE NETWORK

GEERT LOVINK

> In the final stage of his "liberation" and emancipation through the networks, screens and technologies, the modern individual becomes a fractal subject, both subdivisible to infinity and indivisible, closed on himself and doomed to endless identity. In a sense, the perfect subject, the subject without other – whose individuation is not at all contradictory with mass status.[1] *Jean Baudrillard, 1999*

This is the age of network extinction.[2] Small is trivial. The notorious vagueness and non-commitment of their slackerish members almost killed the once-cute postmodern construct of 'networks', and platforms did the rest. Decentralization may be still in favor, but no one is talking about networks as a solution for the mess that social media is in. Where have all the networks gone?

In this age of the subject without a project, there is no 'underground' anymore. Once, building one, two, three, many networks as alternatives to crumbling institutions such as trade unions or political parties was a fashionable post-Cold-War tactic. Back then, networks were seen by shady agencies like the RAND Corporation as stealth-technologies, able to infiltrate, disrupt and penetrate rogue states and/or other actors perceived as enemies of the United States' world order. Following the democratization of the internet, the concept of 'the network' first introduced in the 80s in the field of banking (as 'financial networks') has now reached the status of *gesunkenes Kulturgut.*[3] Was it the 'open', informal character of 'the network' that killed it – or, rather, the absence of a collective will to do anything much more than feed on clickbait?

For *TechCrunch* writer Romain Dillet, the term 'social network' has been emptied of meaning: 'Chances are you have dozens, hundreds or maybe thousands of friends and followers across multiple platforms. But those crowded places have never felt so empty.'[4] He concludes that the concept of wide networks composed of social ties with an element of broadcasting is dead. For Dillet, what killed the network was the never-ending push to add more 'people you may know', on the basis that more equals better, in alignment with the capitalist imperative of perpetual growth. According to this logic of social networks, accumulating more friends is equivalent to a firm demonstrating a strong capacity to expand its market reach. Yet a sad

---

1   Jean Baudrillard, *Impossible Exchange*, London: Verso, 2015 (1999), p. 64.
2   This text was commissioned by transmediale and is a shortened version of the original essay written in July–September 2019. The full version can be found on my blog, net critique, http://networkcultures.org/geert.
3   lit. 'sunken cultural goods', a term coined by folklorist Hans Naumann, which is rarely translated out of the original German.
4   Romain Dillet, 'The Year Social Networks Were No Longer Social – In Praise of Private Communities', *TechCrunch* (23 December 2018), https://techcrunch.com/2018/12/23/the-year-social-networks-were-no-longer-social/. All quotes from this paragraph are from this article.

emptiness accompanies the mass individualization of the cult of personality. Dillet: 'Knowing someone is one thing, but having things to talk about is another.' Blaming the dark pattern design that emerged in the desperate attempt to push even more ads – tech companies will do whatever it takes to grow – Dillet concludes: 'As social networks become bigger, content becomes garbage.' Yet here, instead of entering the political debate on how to break up these monopolies and build meaningful alternative tools that could replace the platforms, for example, Dillet resorts to the making of a cheap 'digital detox' gesture: 'Put your phone back in your pocket and start a conversation. You might end up discussing for hours without even thinking about the red dots on all your app icons.' Is it really so impossible to reimagine the social without blaming ourselves for being weak, addicted individuals?

In the meantime, the term 'networks' has been elegantly removed from the tech vocabulary. Search for the term in the books that capture the current state of the internet, such as Nick Srnicek's *Platform Capitalism* (2015), Benjamin Bratton's *The Stack* (2016) or Shoshana Zuboff's *The Age of Surveillance Capitalism* (2019), and you will search in vain. Not even activist literature uses the term much anymore, and the mathematics- and social-science-driven 'network theory' has been dead for over a decade. In fact, the left never made a notable effort to 'own' the concept; if anyone did, it was 'global civil society', a hand-picked collection of NGOs that played around with Manuel Castells' *Network Society* in an attempt to enter the realm of institutional politics at a transnational level. The distribution of power over networks turned out to be nothing but a dream. The valorization of 'flat hierarchies', a notion especially endorsed by 'the network is the message' advocates, has been replaced by a platform system driven by influencers who are 'followed' in a passive-aggressive mode by everyone else, without consequence. Absent a redistribution of wealth and power, we feverishly continue to 'network' under the calibrated eye of platform algorithms.

So, whatever happened to the network idea? In researching this essay I have made the rounds, consulting with fellow activists, artists and researchers on different continents on how they see the sorry status of networks now. I started out by talking with the Dutch post-digital art critic Nadine Roestenburg, who believes that millennials and Gen-Z see networks as a given:

> [A]n underlying structure that no longer takes a fixed shape. Everybody and everything is always connected to each other, there is no longer a white space between the nodes. The network has exploded into a void; a hyperobject too big, too complex for our understanding. Meaning is lost in meaningfulness and therefore we are desperately searching for a starting point, a single node that can reconnect us. This explains the popularity of digital detoxes, mindfulness, meditation. In [the] arts, psychogeography, as a tool to trace the physical[ity] of the digital, in a requiem for understanding, starting with the visualiz[ation of] the invisible network structure.[5]

Roestenburg then suggested I contact Jenny Odell, the Bay Area-based author of *How to Do Nothing*. Odell wrote back:

5   Email exchange with Nadine Roestenburg, 25 July 2019.

One thing that hasn't changed is that we require certain contexts in order for speech and action to be meaningful. There is such a big difference between 1) saying things in a group where you are recognized, and which has convened (physically or digitally) around a specific purpose; and 2) shouting into an anonymous void, having to package your expressions in a way that will grab the attention of strangers who have no context for who you are and what you're saying. Both in group chats and [at] in-person meetings, I'm amazed at how things actually get *done* rather than just *said*, with people being able to build off of the expertise of others in an atmosphere of mutual respect. Social media, through the process of context collapse, makes this kind of thing impossible by design.[6]

Odell believes it is worth revisiting and defending the idea of decentralized federation,

because the model preserves the aspects of sociality that make the most of the individual and the group. Looking back at the history of activism, the decentralized form shows up over and over again. The density of the nodes allows people to form real relationships, and the connections between the nodes allow them to share knowledge quickly. To me, this represents the possibility of innovating new ideas and solutions – rather than one-off, mic-drop statements and a bunch of "connected" individuals simply spinning their wheels.[7]

Now let's get unfashionable, dig up an Adorno quote from *Critical Models* and recast it into the social media age: 'The old established authorities decayed and were toppled, while the people psychologically were not ready for self-determination. They proved to be unequal to the freedom that fell into their laps.'[8]

This is what networks require: an active form of self-determination. Self-organization from below is the precise opposite of smooth interfaces, automated imports of address books and algorithmic 'governance' of one's news and updates. Self-determination is not something you can download and install for free. During the turbulent 90s, centralized information systems lost their power and legitimacy; but instead of smaller networks that claimed to be more democratic, and – in theory – to promote people's autonomy and sovereignty, all we got was ever larger and more manipulative monopolistic platforms. Self-determination is an act, as it turns out, or a series of actions; a political event, or event-series – and not an inbuilt feature of software.

Like any form of social organization, networks need to be set up, built, and maintained. Unlike what mapping software seems to suggest, networks are not created whole, and on the spot, as if they were machine-generated entities. We're not talking here about automated correlations; forget the visual snapshots. Networks are constituted by protocols and their

6   Email exchange with Jenny Odell, 7 August 2019.
7   Email exchange with Jenny Odell, 7 August 2019.
8   Theodor W. Adorno, *Critical Models: Interventions and Catchwords*, New York: Columbia University Press, 2005, p. 191.

underlying infrastructures. And they're lively, too: once networks start to grow on their own, they may develop in unexpected directions; they may branch off, diverge, flourish but then stagnate, and are just as easily abandoned as they are to get started. Unlike other forms of organization, the political charm of networks lies in their ability to create new beginnings, a miraculous energy much like that which Hannah Arendt describes, when she writes of what is unleashed when we begin anew.[9] Might rethinking networks as tools for re-beginning lure us away from 'collapsology' and our never-ending obsession with the ending of this world?[10]

It may be that the informal character of networks encourages unknown outsiders to join them; however, it is this, too, that can lead to a culture of non-commitment, the formation of informal hierarchies, and power-plays by and among those who are most active in them. What are we supposed to do? Respond? Like? Retweet? This uncertainty is part of the network architecture when you do not have the pseudo-activity of likes, clicks, and views. Networks are easy to join – and to abandon. They require neither formal membership nor the creation of a profile – a random username and password is all that's usually required. But neither do networks just 'fall out of the sky', however events such as riots and flash mobs might seem to suggest otherwise. On platforms, the characteristic ebbs and flows, the ups and downs of networks, are replaced (or overcome) by a constant stream of messages. Instead of inviting us to act, this requires that we spend most of our time keeping up-to-date, in a constant state of mild panic, trying to work through the backlog of tweets and updates we might have missed or ignored over the past few days. Depleted and too wiped out to do anything else, we're left near-comatose, contemplating the now-familiar void. An emptiness amplified by a sense that there's nothing better to do is one of the primary affective consequences of this mass-training for an automated future. Platforms establish a psychic blockade against thinking and acting (to put it in Mark Fisher's terms); their 'service design' is such that we're no longer lured to action, but instead express our outrage or concern. These are the 'networks without a cause' that invite us to respond to each and every event primarily and only with stripped-down opinions, basic responses.

In Italy, a country where the term 'social networks' is still circulating, the debate over the current state of the social is as lively as ever. Writing in response to my thesis on the death of the network in the age of platform capitalism, Tiziana Terranova, author of *Network Cultures* (2004), states her conviction:

> [I]f we can look back at the network age it [is] possible only because we seem to be at the highest point of the network wave – a mathematical abstraction derived from and implemented into communication technologies, which still completely dominates and organizes the epistemic space of contemporary societies. What we probably can look back on, and many of us are [doing], is [a] hopeful time of networks,

9   See Oliver Marchert, *Neu Beginnen*, Wien: Verlag Turia + Kant, 2005, pp. 18-19.
10   'Collapsology is the study of the collapse of industrial civilization and what could succeed it.' The
      concept was developed by Pablo Servigne and Raphaël Stevens in their 2015 essay 'Comment tout tout
      collombrer: Collapsology', *Archeos* (8 January 2019), https://www.archeos.eu/collapsologie/. See also
      Collapsologie, a site that 'keeps track of the scientific literature on ecological collapse, limits to growth
      and existential risks', <www.collapsologie.fr>.

when it was still possible to see new possibilities in the network topos, rather than just the reorganization of power. It might be possible to perceive, even now, what networks might eventually give in to, something emerging at the very limits of hyperconnectedness and the proliferation of correlations that have displaced modern notions of causality. If I had to place a bet on what this something might be, I would put it on technologies that employ quantum-theoretical models of entanglement (rather than connectedness) and "spooky" models of causality. It might be possible that this is where new technologies of power and struggles for emancipation from the grip of economic, social and cultural relations might have to unfold. Translating this within my own framework, I have to think of "unlikely networks" – those constituted not of family, high-school friends and colleagues, but of seemingly random strangers, and via a much weirder and more radical process than those by which algorithms are now selecting partners on dating apps. Event-driven entanglements are important here.[11]

In his 2018 collection of interviews *Facebook entkommen*, the Austrian researcher Raimund Minichbauer neatly sums up the stagnation in which, he claims, numerous artists, activists, and researchers have found themselves since 2011, when the last renaissance of certain social movements occurred, and the last attempts at a certain kind of 'indie' social networking were made before the final lock-in.[12] Much to the surprise of insiders, most autonomous groups and social centers still use Facebook to announce their activities. Informed by similar considerations to those articulated in Minichbauer's publication, the Institute of Network Cultures' *Unlike Us* network embodies a similar attempt to combine social media critique with the promotion of alternatives. Despite two waves of public interest, one after the 2013 revelations of Snowden, the other in the aftermath of the Cambridge Analytica scandal in early 2018, nothing has fundamentally changed. Even though we know a lot more about 'behavior modifications' and the 'abuse' of user data, these insights have not led to a significant change in platform dependencies.

While the list of alternative apps steadily grows, how can activists be so openly cynical about their own alternatives? And what does it say about the level of 'regression' in Western societies, when even the most engaged activists are so 'liberal' about Facebook use? Is it laziness? Is the fear of being isolated otherwise justified? Once upon a time, alternative communication infrastructure was considered vital to the survival of 'the scene': from zines, bookstores, independent distributors, and print shops, to free/pirate radio stations, autonomous internet servers, and related ISPs. Interviewed in *Facebook entkommen* (2018), the data activist/ researcher Stefania Milan describes the move to what she terms 'cloud protesting'. As Milan herself witnessed when the Occupy camp in Toronto was evicted, this is when activists respond to incidents such as police violence by becoming instant reporters, grabbing their phones to document and upload the incriminating evidence to social media platforms. Milan prefers to speak of 'mobilizations' rather than 'movements', and notes the contradiction between the horizontal decision-making structures observed at events by activists, such as

11   Email exchange with Tiziana Terranova, 8 August 2019.
12   Raimund Minichbauer, *Facebook entkommen*, Wien: Transversal Texts, 2018, pp. 101-103.

the 'human microphone' protocol that emerged at Occupy, and the absolute lack of similar structures and/or protocols within the technical infrastructures of the platforms that such 'cloud protestors' utilize.[13]

Minichbauer points at another sensitive issue where social movements, geeks and technology designers appear not to have made any progress: that is, the question of 'community'. Mark Zuckerberg's systematic abuse of the term is on full display whenever he talks about 'his' 2.4 billion Facebook users as if they were one 'global community'.[14] As Minichbauer suggests, it would be easy to dismiss this appropriation of the term, as if we should not persist in deconstructing shallow corporate definitions – but neither should we allow our dismissive aversion to such usage (or to platforms per se) to lead us to take a position in which we reject any form of platform-based mutual aid or (free) cooperation with others out of fear that our every interaction might be – or indeed, is being – tracked, mapped, and commodified. As Haraway says, we should 'stay with the trouble.'[15] Community is either a living entity that exists in the here and now, with all of its contradictions and mishaps, such that 'we' have something in common – a commons, that is – or it is a dead entity that should no longer be invoked while we're in search of other forms of the social. As studies of kinship have shown, many people are glad to escape the strains of close-knit living. As Jon Lawrence has written in *The Guardian*: 'If we abandon vague aspirations to rediscover an idealized vision of community that never existed and focus instead on small-scale, practical initiatives to foster social connection and understanding, we stand a chance of weathering the present crisis with our social fabric intact.'[16]

And Charles Hugh Smith, writing on networks vs. central planning: 'Whether we acknowledge it or not, the world is placing its bets on which system will survive the coming era of destabilizing non-linear change: inflexible, opaque Central Planning [sic] or flexible, self-organizing networks of decentralized autonomy and capital.'[17] This, then, is the choice with which 'we' have failed to see ourselves presented over the past decades: a diverse coalition of liberal business elites, geek entrepreneurs and activists have consistently overlooked the possibility that 'the internet' itself would one day be a Central Planning Committee platform. Having used the network logic in order to advance a ruthless process of hypergrowth at all costs, the collection of entities known as 'Silicon Valley' appears to have dumped the network logic altogether. Once all of our address books were copied, our networks properly 'mapped', their diffuse and 'rhizomatic' structure became a nuisance and was discarded in favor of clearly defined, profile-centric 'graphs', or metrics, of how users interact with products and 'friends'.

13   Minichbauer, *Facebook entkommen*.
14   Mark Zuckerberg, 'Building Global Community', *Facebook* (16 February 2017), https://www.facebook.com/notes/mark-zuckerberg/building-global-community/10154544292806634.
15   Donna J. Haraway, *Staying with the Trouble: Making Kin in the Chthulucene. Experimental Futures*, Durham: Duke University Press, 2016.
16   Jon Lawrence, 'The Good Old Days? Look Deeper and the Myth of Ideal Communities Fades', *Guardian* (11 August 2019), https://www.theguardian.com/commentisfree/2019/aug/11/good-old-days-look-deeper-and-myths-of-ideal-communities-fades.
17   Charles Hugh Smith, 'Which One Wins: Central Planning or Adaptive Networks?', *Of Two Minds* (19 February 2019), https://www.oftwominds.com/blogfeb19/evolution-wins2-19.html.

Strangely enough, the demise of network logic has not (yet) been properly theorized. Meanwhile, networks have become an invisible secondary layer in 'the stack',[18] and a 'remediation' effect (as described by Bolter and Grusin) has come into play: the content of the platform is the network. This only works, however, if the mesh of 'friends' or 'followers' actually constitute active networks. Platforms become worthless if these are fake or dead. Indeed, platforms can only come into being and generate the desired extractive value if there are actual exchanges and interactions happening, on a scale beyond a certain critical mass. Automated exchanges between machines (bots) can simulate the social, but such 'fake' traffic only works to generate value if it exists parasitically, in addition to that of real live users; in isolation from whom they become worthless. Without humans such as sys-admins, moderators, software developers and network maintenance workers, any platform would cease functioning: forget one patch and the whole system breaks down. And while anyone can set up a website, run an app, or host a network, there are still only a very few with the meta-level skills and resources to run a platform.

In Shoshana Zuboff's *The Age of Surveillance Capitalism* (2019), 'the network' isn't even mentioned. Perhaps the term is too drily technical for Zuboff, who prefers to borrow from behavioral science terms for animal-group behaviors such as 'hive' and 'herd'. These, she contrasts with what she claims to be a specifically human need for the 'sanctuary' of the 'home', for, in her own words: 'surveillance capitalism has *human* nature in its sight.'[19] The new frontier of power, for Zuboff, is the data-extraction of the 'behavioral surplus' for repackaging and resale in the form of predictions, for the logic of surveillance capitalism is precisely that of extraction-prediction-modification. Unlike what many artists, theorists and activists once feared, it is not the 'social noise' of our precious informal relations that is appropriated (and so compromised) by machines: the prime targets are minds, brains, and behaviors. For Zuboff, so-called 'social media' are primarily neither social nor mediational in purpose.

The network form, in contrast, embodies a constructivist view of the social as neither a technical protocol nor a mere given, but a vital element or utility of society which continuously requires to be recreated, maintained, and cared for by humans: without this, networks rapidly break down. This is in stark contrast not only with the instrumentalist Silicon Valley view but also those of science & technology (STS) scholars who indulge an admiration for autopoietic automation without cranky wetware threatening to spoil the party, and for whom networks embody the 'all too human': vulnerable, moody, unpredictable, sometimes boring or rather excessive, and yes, sometimes out of control. These network characteristics can all be 'managed' and 'administrated' through moderation, filtering, censorship and 'algorithmic governance'; but they cannot wholly be eliminated 'for good'.

What happens if we start to look at social media from an instrumentalist point of view, and apply this Skinnerian dogma to today's platforms: 'A person does not act upon the world, the world acts upon him'? Against most cultural studies approaches that emphasize the neoliberal

---

18   I further describe this rearrangement of the key terms of 'media', 'network', 'platform', and 'stack' in my book *Sad by Design*, London: Pluto Press, 2019.

19   Shoshana Zuboff, *The Age of Surveillance Capitalism*, London: Profile Books, 2019, p. 346.

subjectivity of the competitive self, for Zuboff there is no more individuality: as part of the herd, we're programmed to do what our digital instinct tells us to. In her classic sociological view (informed by Durkheim), there is little room left for agency: these days, us weakened neoliberal subjects are no longer considered as self-confident actors. The good old days when practitioners of British cultural studies discovered hidden capabilities for subversive appropriation, potential and actual, among apparently passive consumers are over. Now we online billions are frowned upon either as busy bees working for the Valley, or as addicts and victims of the latest conspiracy to manipulate our tastes and opinions. And we urgently need the agency that we lack.

How did this *Netzvergessenheit*, this forgetfulness towards networks, occur? Once, when a network became too big, it was supposed first to disintegrate, then to regroup, then to replicate its structure at a higher, or meta level to create a 'network of networks'. For those around in the 'emerging' 90s, some of these dynamics were patently on display. These days, the foundational network principles — decentralization, distribution, federation — still sound idealistic and magnificent, yet more unreachable than ever before. Historically speaking, the trouble started right at the height of their influence. When the internet population started to grow exponentially in the late 90s to early 00s, diversification reached a critical point, as users started to flock to the same websites. Conceptually speaking, Web 2.0 began with 'scale-free networks' that exhibited a power-law degree of distribution. The introduction of this term marked a paradigmatic shift, indicating the end of the old-school idea that networks simply had an upper size-limit, after which they would fall apart and almost 'naturally' create new nodes.[20] The conceptual step from scale-free networks to 'the platform' was a small one, but it took almost a decade, up until 2010, when Tarleton Gillespie formulated the first rules of what was to become the internet platform economy.

Mathematics-based network science has had its day, and, in any case, remains silent over 'the law of scale-free bullshit'. Most of the engineers who built it all not only remain silent but claim innocence. 8chan founder Fredrick Brenner is one of the few to publicly express second thoughts: 'There's this idea that if we have unbridled freedom of speech that the best ideas will fall out. But I don't really think that's true anymore. I mean, I've looked at 8chan and I've been its admin, and what happens is the most rage-inducing memes are what wins out.'[21]

---

20 See also danah boyd on how her term 'context collapse' emerged in the early Web 2.0 period. danah boyd, 'how "context collapse" was coined: my recollection', *apophenia* (8 December 2013), http://www. zephoria.org/thoughts/archives/2013/12/08/coining-context-collapse.html.

21 Nicky Woolf, 'Destroyer of worlds: How a childhood of anger led the founder of 8chan to create one of the darkest corners of the internet', *Tortoise Media* (29 June 2019), https://members.tortoisemedia. com/2019/06/29/8chan/content.html. See also the work of Alberto Brandolini, originator of the bullshit asymmetry principle; Brandolini's law emphasizes the difficulty of debunking bullshit, the development of the 'intellectual denial of service' concept, and that of 'bad infinitum': 'a tendency for non-experts to overwhelm experts with repetitive costly, and often unproductive demands for evidence or counter-argument to oft-debunked or misleading claims', *Techiavellian*, https://techiavellian.com/intellectual-denial-of-service-attacks.

Similarly, in the case of actor-network theory, it simply could not compute the ugly side of social media platforms. None of this was supposed to happen, even as the political-economy blind-spot of the 'mapping-without-a-cause' Latour school became blatantly evident. From the late 90s onwards, it was increasingly clear that academics and theorists were no longer capable of keeping up with Silicon Valley's hypergrowth strategy, as its venture capitalists quietly financed the move from neoliberal markets to the creation of monopolies by 'breaking things'. Clearly, the wisdom of the few was that competition was for losers. The once remarkable insight that non-human entities such as bots are also actors no longer mattered.

Amsterdam-based student activist and theorist Sepp Eckenhaussen stresses the role of the network as a business model:

> Networks generate data and data equals money. Needless to say, these are not ordinary users. In this model, surplus value is constantly taken out of the network. This is known to be the case with social media but also happens in self-organized solidarity networks. These mechanisms seem to work best where[ever] the isolation of precarious subjects is worse [than elsewhere], and at once also felt most [strongly], such as in the art scene: the longing for community makes us easy prey. The willingness to share freely and build up sincere connections can easily lead to an "enclosure of the commons". Look at how academics ran into the business-trap of academia.edu, after they had uploaded all their work in full confidence that they were sharing it amongst their own network and that it would not be exploited.[22]

Dead or not, let's look into the ongoing potential of networks. Data activist and researcher Niels ten Oever, who works with Stefania Milan on the Datactive project, emphasizes their invisible aspect:

> Networks provide orderings to our lives, societies, machines, and cities. When networks make themselves known, they become visible in an almost burlesque manner: we want to see them, we know they are there, and yet they always remain at least partially covered. They evade total capture, whatever we build on top of networks to make them seem interconnected, centralized, and uniform. Underlying networks show themselves at time of change, rupture, and crisis.[23]

For ten Oever, networks still exist and thrive best underground:

> The network is a complex assemblage, a multiplicity, that has raw and fuzzy edges and never really works as expected. It can never be completely seen or understood. After wreaking havoc on the world, [...] networks cede back to where they belong: underground. Movements that are built on top of networks can have two fates: either they dissipate back into the distributed nature of the network (where they still travel!)

22 Ico Maly, 'The end of Academia.edu: how business takes over, again', *diggit magazine* (22 February 2018), https://www.diggitmagazine.com/column/end-academiaedu-how-business-takes-over-again.
23 Email exchange with Niels ten Oever, 5 August 2019.

or they centralize and get shed by the network itself, where they flow to the logic of institutionalization. Our plans should be big, but our expectations should be low. There is nothing wrong with being underground.[24]

The Euro-American cultural critic Brian Holmes, who has been an active nettime member for over two decades, believes that the network paradigm is still alive:

Here's the thing about the contemporary communications network: each of its human nodes is a socialized individual emerging from deep collective time, whether centuries or millennia. Network theorist Manuel Castells was spectacularly wrong: the Net and the Self are not ontologically opposed, but instead, they're continually intertwined at all levels. This means that if you want a network to successfully self-organize, its members have to develop both an explicit ethics and a shared cultural horizon, as to overcome the inherited frameworks of belief and behaviour. Anarchists already knew this in practice, since their communities typically involve some kind of overarching philosophical dimension, as well as carefully articulated codes for daily collective life. At the opposite end of the political spectrum, Islamist radicals knew it too: they called on ancient religious beliefs and updated sharia laws to knit their networks together. That's why such groups could successfully take the lead during the early rounds of networked politics, beginning in 1999 and 2001 respectively. Meanwhile, media theorists including myself were projecting the idea that as long as you built it with free software, the computer-linked media system represented a clean break with the past: a sudden liberation from the manipulated corporate channels that had blocked spontaneous self-organization for so long. And here's the other thing: it just wasn't true.[25]

Holmes also believes we still live in networked societies:

I still spend a lot of time working on technological platforms for self-organizing nets, such as the map/geoblog I'm currently making for the Anthropocene River network. What's clear, however, is that networked cultures aren't born from technological inventions such as the microprocessor or TCP/IP. Instead, they are made by individuals working collectively to transform not just their technological tools, but also their cultural horizons, and above all their day-to-day codes of ethical conduct. How to accomplish such profound cultural and philosophical work while still attending to the complex technologies on which most everyday social interactions now depend? That's where the political question is coalescing right now.[26]

The precarity theorist from Milan Alex Foti thinks that 'the distinction [between the] technical [network and the] social network has now blurred as the political and ethical

24   Email exchange with Niels ten Oever, 5 August 2019.
25   Email exchange with Brian Holmes, 7 August 2019.
26   Email exchange with Brian Holmes, 7 August 2019.

aspects of algorithmic technology have come to the fore.'[27] He urges us to form our own platform parties and organizations, because:

> [I]solated individuals on social media are less powerful than party cabals that resort to bot armies and constant media manipulation. Online platforms are the only way to grow fast in membership and power. Federalism is at the heart of the European project, but that doesn't equate with horizontalism. We need to have a federal republic of Europe, federated hackers of the Union, federated collectives of xenofeminists, etc. It's time for effectiveness over righteousness. Anti-systemic forces need intellectual debate but also a shared line, and especially disciplined local cadres ready to fight for the planet against fossil capitalism. This means developing a green anti-capitalist ideology that gives meaning to the struggles of people and an organization that embodies it and implements it, especially if civil wars break out after ecological catastrophe.[28]

What emerges out of the patchwork of experiences of the past decades is a new notion of network-driven techno-voluntarism. Forget automated processes, compulsory updates. The strength of a network is not to *inform* its participants – information does not lead to action. This takes us back to the core question of the organization of like-minded souls that come together to take action, and all of the related assumptions that need to be taken apart. How do such 'cells' come into being? Can we overcome paranoia and a lack of trust of strangers, and start to act with 'the Other' in ways that open up filter bubbles in order to establish cosmopolitan platforms that facilitate local networks for working together on, yes, the peer-to-peer production of common care? We know how to exchange information, how to communicate; now what need is to put this knowledge to use in cause-based contexts. We don't need no more updates.

The European counter-meme collective Clusterduck lists the following tactics for the defense of networks:

> Our digital communities constantly undergo forms of intrusion, pollution, appropriation. Networks are not dead and yet they are buried. The right to network is not granted and must be claimed through practices of analysis, hijacking and reappropriation. From the BBS frontiers to Web 2.0, the human capacity for cooperation has constantly evolved, defying easy definitions.
>
> Surviving as a network today requires an increasingly complex toolkit of practices: creating a movement based on a Twitter hashtag to convey a sense of a constant URL activity; hijacking the YouTube RetroPlayer-algorithm to make sure that right-wing commentators' videos are followed by debunking videos capable of bringing radicalized users out of the so-called "alt-right funnel"; organizing moments where the networks can meet IRL to coordinate, celebrate and strengthen the ties between

---

27 Email exchange with Alex Foti, 28 August 2019.
28 Email exchange with Alex Foti, 28 August 2019.

users; founding and administrating thematic groups on mainstream social platforms such as Facebook and Reddit, to lure users and communities away from there and redirect them to fringe social platforms such as Mastodon, Discord or Telegram; analyzing the history of web communities and subcultures, to learn their networking techniques and proceed backwards, in order to understand the processes of hostile appropriation, co-optation and hijacking they had to endure; breaking the cycles of hatred, triggered by bots and sponsored trolls, through white-hat trolling and debunking activities, to turn the quarrel and noise of "reverse censorship" into something meaningful; using contemporary design and codes to carry our messages, and create memes and memetic narratives that can propagate through filter bubbles, in order to bring together communities that would never meet otherwise; exploring new narratives, highlighting the importance of interspecies cooperation and the significance of symbiotic and parasitic relationships in shaping our capacity to co-evolve. "None of us is stronger than all of us" has never been so alive.[29]

All this leaves me with the question of how *I* look (back) at networks. Am I ready to salvage the name of my research institute – the Institute of Network Cultures – to make a statement? Is this a requiem without consequence, like a sing-along song that sticks with you for a while and then gets forgotten? Should I let go, or do I have some emotional attachment to the term? If the concept no longer works, then should it just be dropped? It is true that over the past decade our Institute of Network Cultures has not started up 'a platform' – maybe we should have. Instead, what I have tried to do is to strengthen the concept of the network from within, in order to overcome the indecisive nature of networks. Since 2005, I have worked together with Ned Rossiter on the idea of 'organized networks'. Our book *Organization After Social Media,* in which we brought together our theses, came out in 2018.[30] In it, we deliberately did not address how to scale up with networks. Instead, we propose that the problem of 'weak links' might be overcome by leaving behind the diffuse networks of which they are a feature and working only with much smaller, dedicated online groups that are based on 'strong links'. Against the proclaimed ease of reaching critical mass in no time, and the contemporary desire to go from 'zero to hero' in a day, we put forward the idea of an avant-garde cell or think-tank that sticks to the issue at hand. The shift here is one towards organizations that need certain tools to get things done.

Organized networks invent new institutional forms whose dynamics, properties and practices are internal to the operational logic of communication media and digital technologies. Their emergence is prompted, in part, by wider social fatigue with, and increasing distrust of, institutions such as churches, political parties, firms and labor unions, which maintain hierarchical modes of organization. While not without hierarchical tendencies (founders, technical architectures, centralized infrastructures, personality cults), organized networks do tend to gravitate more strongly toward horizontal modes of communication, practice and planning. Organized networks emerge at times of intense crisis (social, economic, environmental), when dominant institutions fail in their core task: decision-making. As

---

29   Statement by the Clusterduck collective, 17 August 2019.
30   Geert Lovink and Ned Rossiter, *Organization After Social Media*, Colchester: Minor Compositions, 2018.

experiments in collective practice conjoined with digital communication technologies, organized networks are test beds for the networked forms of governance that may strive to address our world's rapid spiral into a planetary abyss.

Is the platform the historically necessary next step, or is it, rather, an anomaly? If tech ubiquity is a given for the foreseeable future, how should we read 1990s-network nostalgia? Is a renaissance of decentralized infrastructure, actively owned and defended by communities, a viable option? What happens if we decide to put in a massive effort to dismantle 'free' platforms and their cultures of subconscious comfort, and distribute actual tools, along with the knowledge of how to use and maintain them? Tech has become a vital part of our social life, and should not be outsourced. This can only be overcome if priority is given to 'digital literacy' (which has gone down the drain over the past decade). Societies pay a high price for the ease of smartphones. Soon, few will be able to afford the inbuilt vagueness of the network logic. Coordination is required, as are debates with consequences. So far, social media have grossly neglected the development of democratic decision-making software. Roaming aimlessly online will increasingly come to seem uninteresting; the ultimate critique of social media platforms will be that they are boring. We're not there yet, but the call to exodus grows louder. There will be more urgent and exciting things to be done: Which tools will bring us closer to the bliss of action?

Networks are not destined to remain inward-looking autopoietic mechanisms. Once situations are on the move, we can no longer distinguish network from event, nor which came first — let's leave such questions to the data analysts (aka historians).

In *The Mushroom at the End of the World*, Anna Lowenhaupt Tsing asks: 'How does a gathering become a "happening", that is, greater than a sum of its parts? One answer is contamination. We are contaminated by our encounters; they change who we are as we make way for others. As contamination changes world-making projects, mutual worlds — and new directions — may emerge.'[31]

---

31   Anna Lowenhaupt Tsing, *The Mushroom at the End of the World*, Princeton: Princeton University Press, 2017, p. 27.

OTHER GEOMETRIES

FEMKE SNELTING

OTHER GEOMETRIES

FEMKE SNELTING

Editors note: This article was originally published in the Affective Infrastructures issue of the transmediale journal.[1] In the run up of its 2019 edition, transmediale hosted the transdisciplinary Study Circle Affective Infrastructures which over a two-month period convened in workshops and online discussions, culminating in public events at the festival. Thinking with several non-circular topologies that emerge from collective desire and action, Femke Snelting recounts and reflects on this experience.

'I want to find a way in this conversation to not remain circling around feelings of powerlessness and stunted outrage; we need "affective infrastructures" that help us feel differently, such that we might act unexpectedly. That we might act at all.' With this call, Lou Cornum opened the archipelagic exchange published in this same journal, now three months ago.[2] Lou invited the Study Circle to explore the dynamic tensions between 'affect' and 'infrastructure' in order to find a way out of the paralyzing feeling of 'circling around'.

A circle is a simple geometric shape. The term 'circle' can refer to the outline of a figure, or to a round shape, including its interior. Circles are mathematically defined as the set of all points in a plane that are at the same distance from a shared center; its boundary or circumference is formed by tracing the curve of a point that keeps moving at a constant radius from the middle.

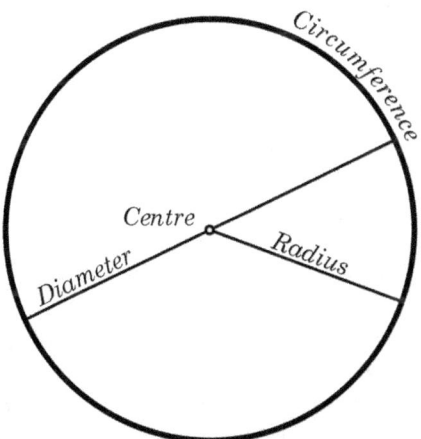

Fig. 1: Circle: diagram. OptImager, Wikimedia Commons (2005), CC BY-SA 3.0.

1   Femke Snelting, 'Other Geometries', *transmediale journal* 3 (2019), https://transmediale.de/content/
     other-geometries.
2   Lou Cornum, in: 'Affective Infrastructures: A Tableau, Altar, Scene, Diorama, or Archipelago',
     transmediale journal 3 (2019).

Circles are omnipresent in practices and imaginaries of collectivity. However, their usefulness for thinking and moving with the kind of 'aspirational ambivalence'[3] that the Study Circle was committed to, is limited. Their flatness provides little in the way of vocabulary for more complex relational notions that attempt to include space, matter and time, let alone interspecies mingling and other uneasy alliances. The obligation to always stay at the same distance from the center promises a situation of equality but does so by conflating it with similarity. Circles divide spaces into an interior and an exterior, a binary separation that is never easy to overcome. We urgently need other axes to move along.

The stage for the Study Circle had been set with a quote from Lauren Berlant in which she introduces the combinatory concept 'Affective Infrastructures' as a way to think about what could bind us together in troubling times. In her text, Berlant takes on the complex project of thinking a commons beyond the objective equivalency of 'likeness'. Her proposal is to actualize resilient structures that could work from and with 'non-sovereign relationality as the foundational quality of being in common'. In other words, she asks us to think with other geometries of relation.

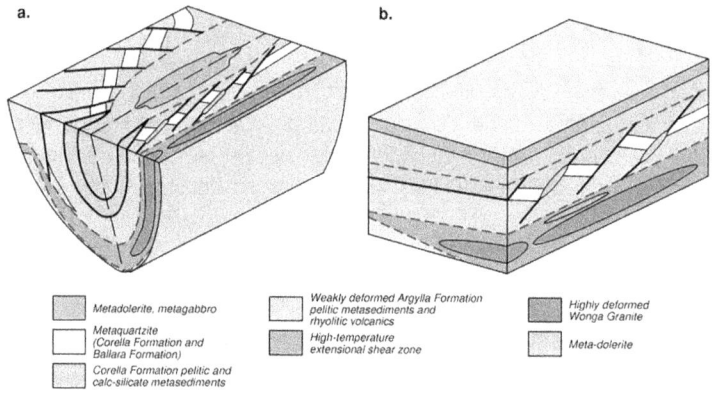

Fig. 2: Folded rock units: separated stratigraphy in upper and lower plates and restored to pre-folding configuration. In: Basin architecture and crustal evolution in the Paleoproterozoic—a field guide for the Rodinia conference (2017).

The *Affective Infrastructures* Study Circle never formed or performed a circle, beyond its very name. Its complex shape was carefully composed by inviting eight geographically dispersed people, speaking and writing through many languages with varying levels of comfort. Our diverse gender realities, geopolitical situations, disciplinary backgrounds, practical experiences and even age differences meant that we each came with specific questions regarding both 'affect' and 'infrastructure'.

---

3   Lauren Berlant, 'The Commons: Infrastructures for Troubling Times', *Environment and Planning D: Society and Space* 34.3 (2016): 393-419.

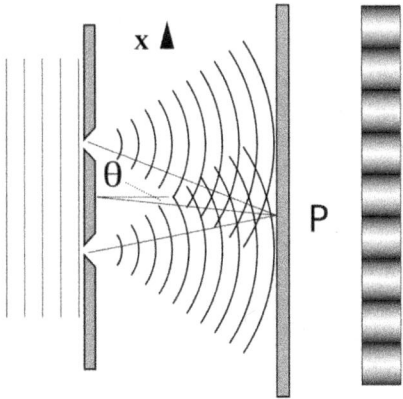

Fig. 3: Diffraction: destructive and constructive interference patterns. Lacatosias, Stanner, Epzcaw, Wikimedia Commons (2018), CC BY-SA 3.0.

The circularity of the Study Circle was further interfered with by overlapping presences, concerns, and tools. A few months before the festival took place, and the day after the elections in Brazil, some of us physically met in Berlin, while others connected remotely online. As gas canisters were thrown at migrants trying to cross border between the U.S. and Mexico, we tried to come to terms with the consequences for ourselves and our allies of Jair Bolsonaro having been elected president. We rallied against political inertia in the face of climate change and battled institutional and gender violence. We communicated across multiple time zones, from three continents, with the help of a mailing list, private email and messaging, video conferencing tools and many online notepads. There were erratic sleep cycles, exhaustion, and personal anxiety; there were network issues and failed connections. There were misunderstandings, surprising discoveries, and quite some funny jokes too. Meanwhile visas expired, and family members, deadlines, and dogs needed to be taken care of.

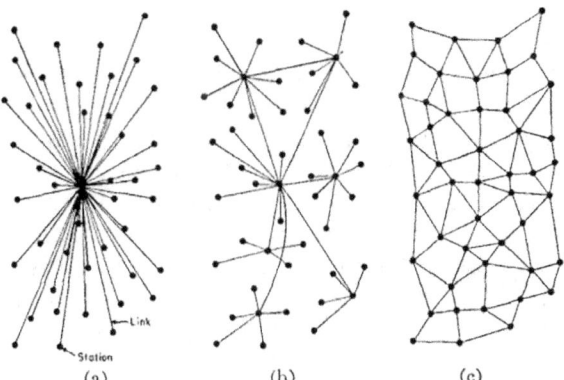

Fig. 1—(a) Centralized. (b) Decentralized. (c) Distributed networks.

Fig. 4: Networks: Paul Baran, On Distributed Networks (1964).

Amidst our scattered connections, other geometries of togetherness start to emerge. Some are explicit, well-known configurations and others more opaque, drifting slowly to the surface. We briefly consider the possibilities of distributed networks. Their iconic representation shows them as the final step in an evolution, neatly ordered along the increasing autonomy and resilience of individual nodes. Distributed networks are a product of Cold War engineering and graphically argue that they continue to perform even after a portion of nodes are incapacitated in an attack. Distributed networks rely on load-balancing sovereign agencies that exert power over others. The defensive drawing does not tell us much about the possibilities for non-sovereign relationality; the kind of infrastructural renderings that we want to converse with need to be less one-dimensional and overly schematic. Our intertwining bibliography orients towards queer, postcolonial and feminist theory, but also fiction. The torsions and tensions that we try to formulate with find companionship in work that affirmatively critiques the regimes of the normative, the legible, and the regular.

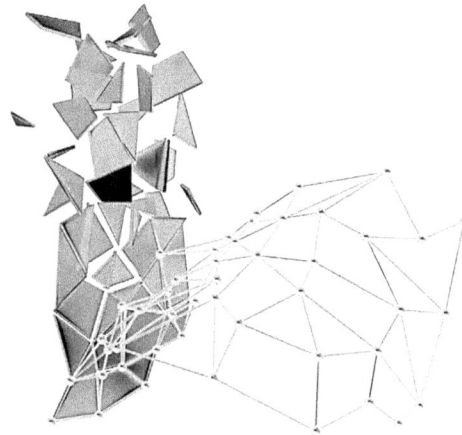

Fig. 5: Paranodes: the negative space of networks. In: Zach Blas, Contra-Internet Inversion Practice #3: Modeling Paranodal Space (2016).

What happens between nodes and edges? Zach Blas invites us to deplace our attention to the negative space of networks, and to stop focusing on the centralizing force of connecting points. Thinking with Ulises Mejias, Blas calls this space 'paranodal', a paradigm shift which makes thinkable 'that which is not only outside the network but also beyond the form of the network itself.'[4] His proposal for paranodal spaces resonates with Nepantla, the locus of resistance that Gloria Anzaldúa makes emerge in Borderlands/La Frontera: The New Mestiza: 'Nepantlas are places of constant tension, where the missing or absent pieces can be summoned back, where transformation and healing may be possible, where wholeness is just out of reach but seems attainable.'[5]

---

4   Zach Blas, 'Contra-Internet', e-flux Journal 74 (June 2016), https://www.e-flux.com/journal/74/59816/
      contra-internet/.
5   Gloria Anzaldúa, Light in the Dark/Luz en lo Oscuro: Rewriting Identity, Spirituality, Reality, Durham:

How to disentangle our experiences of stunted outrage from being caught in the middle of universalist totalitarian apparatuses provided by the GAFAM amalgam? Their homogenizing techno-political framework make dark alignments between modernism, heteropatriarchy, capitalism, and colonialism resurface. Their ongoing promises of equality-through-variability, of optimized affect and monetized relations, make it increasingly difficult to think opacity, contingency, ambiguity and dirty futures beyond yet new ways of exerting power over others (either in the shape of ownership, parenthood, law, species, gender or state). We really need to bend our infrastructural desires in other directions.

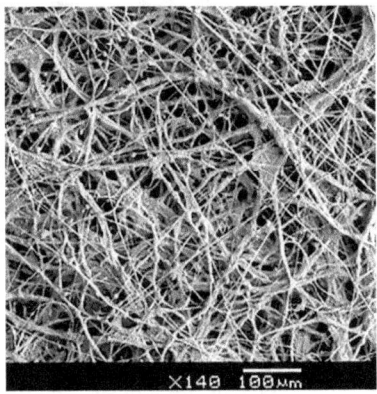

Fig. 6: Mycellium: overlapping mushroom root structure. Sue Van Hook, microscopic imaging (2016)

It is here that the fungal arrives in our conversation as a way to conceptualize non-uniform collaborations under conditions of precarity. Being more than rhizomatic, molds and mycellia seem to mingle effectively with toxic soil, damaged trees, and polluted air as if they were ambitious employees at an afterwork cocktail party. For a fungal infrastructure, contamination is definitely part of the equation. These hypertextual naturecultures also remind us of the fact that the mixing of layers can be violent and not necessarily a voluntary affair. With Anna Lowenhaupt Tsing we wonder how such messy geometries can be responsible with extraction, without reverting to mere calculation. It is curious, how hard it is to draw such non-romantic forms of togetherness.[6]

Duke University Press, 2015, p. 2.

6   Anna Lowenhaupt Tsing, *The Mushroom at the End of the World On the Possibility of Life in Capitalist Ruins*, Princeton, NJ: University Press, 2017.

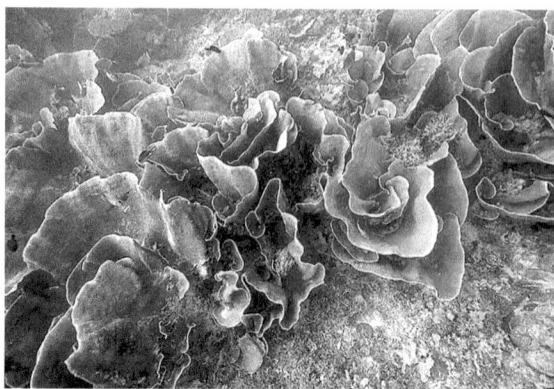

Fig. 7: Lettuce coral: at a deeper location, more discoidal leaves form. Scott Boyd, Palau (2006)

We jump from the de-stratifying scum of fungi to the alluring promises of hyperbolic geometry through the generous folds of the carrier bag, from inside to outside and back again. 'A leaf a gourd a shell a net a bag a sling a sack a bottle a pot a box a container. A holder. A recipient.'[7] Ursula K. Le Guin enlists multiple images of envelopment and asks us to consider structures that can hold together extra-equal agencies. Her porous containers vibrate with Berlants' call for non-sovereign relationality and make a diffractive topology of interconnected surfaces appear. Could the swooping dimensionality of Affective Infrastructures curl up the parallel postulates of solid planes?[8]

And then, there is the tidal imaginary of the archipelago. With Édouard Glissant we wonder about networks of relations in a state of permanent transformation. Our affective infrastructural imaginations are being moved by the unpredictable combination of changing currents, a hot breeze and the shifting landscape of many islands. They diffract together in a *métissage* without limits; maybe this is not another geometry but a different world altogether? 'Archipelagic thought is well suited to the ways of our world. It draws from its ambiguity, its fragility, its derivation. It is in accordance with the practice of the detour, which is not the same as flight or resignation.[9]

Our ongoing experience of knotting together different scales and intensities, without attempting to collapse them into each other, made increasingly clear that in order to rise to the challenge of thinking 'affect' with 'infrastructure' we needed to connect the *how* and *what* of the Study Circle. Dispersion, insecurity, precarity, suspension, instability, difference... How to think through and with the constraints of non-circular togetherness?

7   Ursula K. Le Guin, 'The Carrier Bag Theory of Fiction', in Cheryll Glotfelty and Harold Fromm (eds) *The Ecocriticism Reader: Landmarks in Literacy Ecology*, Athens, Georgia: University of Georgia Press, 1996 [1988], pp. 149-154, p. 150.
8   'Rolling inward enables rolling outward; the shape of life's motion traces a hyperbolic space, swooping and fluting like the folds of a frilled lettuce, coral reef, or bit of crocheting.' Donna Haraway, *Staying with the Trouble: Making Kin in the Chthulucene*, Durham: Duke University Press, 2016, p. 68.
9   Édouard Glissant, *Traité du Tout-Monde: Poétique IV*, Paris: Gallimard, 1997, p. 31. Translation by author.

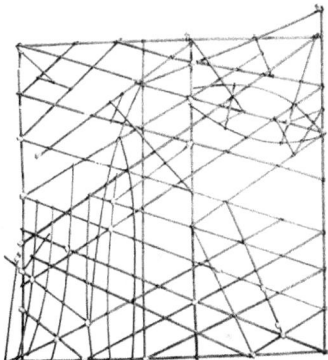

Fig. 8: Stick chart: Polynesian navigation device showing directions of winds, waves and islands. S. Percy Smith (1904).

When The Study Circle shared its thoughts at a public discussion, we were asked if we had any ideas how to implement the dynamic tensions between 'affect' and 'infrastructure' into actual tools and software. Our replies were hesitant; not because we wanted to negate the importance of concretization, but because to imagine togetherness with difference, we first need to change our frames of reference to ones that do not depend on zero eccentricity. This shifting of geometries is a necessary step to come up with technological renderings of possible non-utopian models that go beyond the rigidifying assumptions of sameness and reciprocity. If affective infrastructures have any capacity for providing us with the means for acting at all, they will need to be simultaneously complex and concrete, or they will not be.[10]

10   Private conversation with Jara Rocha, 2019.

SEVEN THESES ON THE FEDIVERSE AND THE BECOMING OF FLOSS

AYMERIC MANSOUX AND
ROEL ROSCAM ABBING

SEVEN THESES ON THE FEDIVERSE AND THE BECOMING OF FLOSS

AYMERIC MANSOUX AND ROEL ROSCAM ABBING

Meet the Fediverse

In recent years, in the context of sustained criticism and general fatigue that surrounds large-scale corporate social media platforms,[1] the desire to build alternatives has grown stronger. This has manifested through the emergence of a wide range of projects, driven by various motives. These projects introduce themselves by emphasizing what makes them distinct from corporate social media, whether it is their ethics, their organizational structure, their underlying technologies, their features, their source code access, or the special interest communities they seek to support. Although diverse, these platforms tend to have one common purpose: to directly question the vendor lock-in of the dominant social media landscape. As a result, they call for different levels of decentralization and interoperability in terms of network architectures and data circulation. These platforms are colloquially known as the 'Fediverse', a portmanteau of 'federation' and 'universe'. Federation is a concept derived from political theory in which various actors that constitute a network decide to cooperate collectively. Power and responsibility are distributed as they do so. In the context of social media, federated networks exist as different communities on different servers that can interoperate with each other, rather than existing as a single software or single platform. This idea is not new, but it has recently gained traction and revitalized efforts toward building alternative social media.[2]

Earlier attempts to create federated social media platforms came from Free/Libre and Open Source Software (FLOSS) communities.[3] They traditionally had an interest in providing *libre* alternatives to existing closed source and proprietary software. As such, these projects were originally promoted as similar in function to the corporate platforms but made with FLOSS. As they were mostly articulated around the openness of protocols and source code, these software platforms catered to a limited audience of users and software developers, who were largely concerned with issues typical of FLOSS culture. This lack of reach changed in 2016 with the introduction of Mastodon, a combination of client and server software for federated social media. Mastodon was quickly adopted by a diverse community of users, including many people usually under-represented in FLOSS: women, people of color, and queer-identifying people. Upon joining Mastodon, these less-represented communities questioned the social

---

1   See Geert Lovink, *Sad by Design: On Platform Nihilism*, London: Pluto Press, 2019.
2   Throughout this text we use 'corporate social media' and 'alternative social media' as defined in Robert W. Gehl, 'The Case for Alternative Social Media', *Social Media + Society* 1.2 (22 September 2015), https://journals.sagepub.com/doi/pdf/10.1177/2056305115604338.
3   Danyl Strype, 'A Brief History of the GNU Social Fediverse and "The Federation"', *Disintermedia*, 1 April 2017, https://www.coactivate.org/projects/disintermedia/blog/2017/04/01/a-brief-history-of-the-gnu-social-fediverse-and-the-federation.

dynamics of existing FLOSS environments, as well as started to contribute both code and critique, which challenged the dominant one-size-fits-all narrative of corporate social media. It is no coincidence that this shift happened in the wake of Gamergate[4] in 2014, with the rise of the 'alt-right', and the 2016 US presidential elections. By the end of 2017, Mastodon counted more than one million users who wanted to try out the Fediverse as an alternative to corporate social media platforms. There, they could test for themselves whether or not a different infrastructure would lead to different discourses, cultures, and safe spaces.

Today the Fediverse is comprised of more than 3.5 million accounts distributed over almost 5,000 servers, referred to as 'instances', which use software projects such as Friendica, Funkwhale, Hubzilla, Mastodon, Misskey, PeerTube, PixelFed, and Pleroma, to name a few.[5] Most of these instances can be interconnected and are often focused on a specific practice, ideology, or professional activity. In view of this, the Fediverse demonstrates that a shift from universal gigantic social networks to small interconnected instances is not just technically possible, it also responds to a concrete need.

The current popularity of the Fediverse can be seen to be driven by two parallel tendencies. First, an interest in engaging with specific technical choices and concerns about closed protocols and proprietary platforms. Second, a wider willingness to recover agency as users of social media infrastructures. More specifically, while corporate social media platforms have allowed many to publish content online, the biggest impact of Web 2.0 has been the apparent decoupling of matters of infrastructure from matters of social organization. The mix of operating systems and social systems from which net culture first emerged,[6] has been replaced by a system of limited user permissions and privileges. Those who engage with the Fediverse work to undo this decoupling. They want to contribute to network infrastructures that are more honest about their underlying ideologies. These infrastructures do not hide behind manipulative or delusional exploits of ideas like openness, universal access, or apolitical engineering. Although today it is too early to tell whether or not the Fediverse will live up to the expectations of its inhabitants, and how it will impact FLOSS in the long run, it is already possible to map current transformations, as well as the challenges faced in this latest episode of the never-ending saga of net and computational culture. To do so, we present seven theses on the Fediverse and the becoming of FLOSS, in the hope of opening up discussions around some of their most pressing issues.

---

4   For an exploration of #GamerGate and toxic technocultures, see Adrienne Massanari, '#Gamergate and The Fappening: How Reddit's Algorithm, Governance, and Culture Support Toxic Technocultures', *New Media & Society* 19.3 (2016): 329-346.

5   Due to its distributed nature it is not easy to get exact numbers on the amount of users but a few projects do exist that try to quantify the network: The Federation, https://the-federation.info; Fediverse Network https://fediverse.network; Mastodon Users, *Bitcoin Hackers*, https://bitcoinhackers.org/@mastodonusercount.

6   For an example of such early relationship, see Michael Rossman, 'Implications of Community Memory', *SIGCAS – Computers & Society* 6.4 (1975): 7-10.

1. The Fediverse as the Transition from Meme Wars to Network Wars

We acknowledge that any good reflection on net culture today must address memes in one way or another. But what can be added to the discussion of memes in 2020? It seems that everything has already been argued, countered, and overexploited by both academics and artists. What else is left to do apart from constantly keeping up with new meme types and their meanings? One often overlooked point is that, crucially, memes do not exist in a vacuum. There are systems that enable their circulation and amplification: social media platforms.

Social media platforms have taken the democratization of meme production and circulation to a previously unseen scale. Moreover, these platforms have grown in symbiosis with internet meme culture. Corporate social media platforms have been optimized and engineered to favor material with memetic qualities. This material encourages reaction and recirculation and is part of a strategy of user retention and participation in surveillance capitalism. Consequently, in the environments used today for the vast majority of online communication, almost everything has become a meme, or needs to exhibit memetic properties to survive – or be visible – in the universe of algorithmic timelines and feeds informed by metrics.[7]

Given that social media is geared toward communication and interaction, what was completely underestimated was how memes would become far more than either strategically engineered vessels to plant ideas, or funny viral things to share with peers. They became a language, a slang, a collection of signs and symbols through which cultural and subcultural identity could materialize. The circulation of such memes has in turn strengthened certain political discourses, which has become a growing concern for the platforms. Indeed, to maximize the exploitation of their user activity, corporate social media platforms must find the right balance between laissez-faire and regulation. They try to do so by means of algorithmic filtering, community feedback, and terms of services. The corporate platforms are increasingly faced, however, with the fact that they have created Petri dishes for all sorts of opinions and beliefs to circulate out of control, in spite of their efforts to reduce and shape discursive, user-generated content toward inoffensive, business-friendly, and otherwise trivial material. Regardless of what these platforms pretend in PR campaigns or hearings in front of legislators, it is clear that no amount of tech solutionism and no amount of outsourced precarious work by traumatised human moderators[8] will help them to get back into full control.

As a result of increased policing of corporate social media platforms, all those excluded from or harmed in these environments have become further interested in migrating to other platforms that they might control for themselves. The reasons for migrating vary. LGBTQ-affiliated groups seek safe spaces to avoid online bullying and harassment. White supremacists look for platforms where their interpretation of free speech goes unchallenged. Raddle, a radical

---

7   Aymeric Mansoux, 'Surface Web Times', *MCD* 69 (2013): 50-53.
8   Burcu Gültekin Punsmann, 'What I learned from three months of Content Moderation for Facebook in Berlin', *SZ Magazin*, 6 January 2018, https://sz-magazin.sueddeutsche.de/internet/three-months-in-hell-84381.

left Reddit clone, grew out of the ban of its original Reddit forum; on the far-right, there is Voat, another Reddit clone.[9] Both developed their own FLOSS platform as a response to their exclusion. While access to source code, and FLOSS in general is valued in all these efforts, one of the key historical advantage of FLOSS practice is surprisingly ignored: the ability to benefit from and build upon each other's work. What seems to matter now is to write the same software for a limited audience, making sure the source code is not tainted with contributions from another community. This is a new development within FLOSS communities, who have often argued that their work is apolitical.[10] This is why, if we're going to talk about memes today, we must talk about these social media platforms. We must talk about these environments that allow, for better or worse, the sedimentation of knowledge: what happens when a specific discourse accumulates online, the kind of community it attracts and fosters, via the feedback loops by which memetic assemblages form. We must talk about how this process is both enabled by, and impacts the perception of FLOSS.

Corporate social media platforms have decided to cut anything that could endanger their business, while remaining ambivalent about their claim of neutrality. But unlike the radical exodus and software-writing exile of some communities, the Fediverse offers instead a vast system in which communities can be independent while still interfacing with others over several servers. In a situation where either censorship or isolated exodus were the only options, federation opens a third way. It allows a community to engage with exchanges or have conflicts with other platforms while remaining true to its own scope, ideology, and interests. From here, two new scenarios are possible: One, where a localized online culture could be established and appropriated as part of the circulation of discourse within a shared communication network. Two: where radicalized memetic material would likely favor the emergence of thinking along axes of friends and enemies spread across instances, to the extent that simplistic meme wars and propaganda would be replaced with network wars.

2. The Fediverse as an Ongoing Critique of Openness

The concepts of openness, universality, and the free circulation of information have been central narratives for promoting technological progress and growth on the internet and the web. While these narratives have been instrumental in advocating FLOSS and free culture, they have also been crucial in the development of social media, where the goal was to create ever-growing networks, encompassing evermore people, freely communicating with one another. Following liberal traditions, this approach was believed to favor productive exchanges of opinions by providing ample space for free speech, access to more information, and the possibility for anyone to participate. However, these open systems were also open to capture by the market and exposed to the predatory culture of corporations. In the case of the web, this has led to business models that make use of both the structures and the content circulating

---

9   For source code, see Raddle, https://raddle.me/; Postmill, 'GitLab', https://gitlab.com/postmill/Postmill;
     Voat, https://voat.co/; Voat, 'GitLab', https://github.com/voat/voat.
10   Gabriella Coleman, 'The Political Agnosticism of Free and Open Source Software and the Inadvertent
     Politics of Contrast', *Anthropological Quarterly* 77.3 (2004): 507-519.

across the network.[11] Fast forward to now: corporate social media leads in the surveillance of individuals and the prediction of their behavior, in order to convince them to buy into both products and political ideas.

Historically, alternative social media projects such as GNU Social, and more precisely Identi. ca/StatusNet, sought to salvage this situation by creating platforms that tackled this particular form of well-marketed openness. They created interoperating systems explicitly opposed to advertising and tracking. In doing so, they hoped to prove that it is still possible to have an ever-growing network while distributing responsibility over the ownership of data, and in theory to provide the means for various communities to appropriate the platforms' source code and contribute to protocol design. This was pretty much the shared belief in the Fediverse around 2016. This belief remained unchallenged because the Fediverse at the time had not changed much from its early days as a FLOSS social media federation project, started more than a decade before. Consequently, it was made up of a largely homogenous crowd, whose interests intersected technology, FLOSS, and anti-corporate ideologies. However, as the Fediverse's population grew more diverse when Mastodon attracted more heterogeneous communities, conflicts emerged between these different communities. This time it was the Fediverse's own idea of openness that was increasingly challenged by the newcomers. As part of this critique, a call emerged within the user community of Mastodon for the ability to block or 'defederate' with other servers in the Fediverse. Blocking means that users or administrators of servers could choose to prevent content from other servers in the network from reaching them. 'Defederation' in this sense became an additional option in the toolkit for strong community-based moderation, since it prevented confrontation with unwanted or harmful content.

At first the introduction of defederation caused a lot of friction with users of other Fediverse software. Frequent complaints that Mastodon was 'breaking the federation' underscored how the move was seen as a threat to the entire network.[12] In this view, the bigger and more interconnected the network could become, the more successful it might be as an alternative to corporate social media. Similarly, many saw blocking as limiting the possibilities for personal expression and the productive exchange of ideas, fearing filter bubbles and isolation as a consequence. By striving for selected disconnection and challenging the very idea that online discourse is necessarily generative, the communities advocating for defederation also challenged the broader liberal assumptions about openness and universality on which prior Fediverse software was built.

The fact that concurrently to these developments, the Fediverse grew from 200,000 to over 3.5 million accounts, at the time of writing, is unlikely to be a coincidence. Rather than thwarting the network, defederation, self-governing communities, and the rejection of universality

---

11   For a more thorough discussion on the multifaceted enabling aspect of openness but also a comment on openwashing, see Jeffrey Pomerantz and Robin Peek, 'Fifty Shades of Open', *First Monday* 21.5 (2016), https://firstmonday.org/ojs/index.php/fm/article/view/6360/5460.

12   As an example of the discourse against defederating see the comment by Kaiser to the blog entry by robek 'rw' world, 'Mastodon Social Is THE Twitter Alternative For...', *Robek World*, 12 January 2017, https://robek.world/internet/mastodon-social-is-the-twitter-alternative-for/.

allowed the Fediverse to accommodate even more communities. The presence of different servers representing very distinct communities that each have their local culture and agency over their own slice of the network, without being isolated from the larger whole, is one of the more interesting aspects of the Fediverse. However, almost one million of the total number of accounts are the result of the alt-right platform Gab switching to the Fediverse protocols, which shows that the network is still open to capture or domination by a single large party.[13] At the same time, this development immediately triggered a variety of efforts to strengthen the possibilities for servers to deal with this risk of domination. For example, the possibility for some server implementations to federate based on white lists, which allows servers to interconnect on an opt-in rather than opt-out basis. Another proposed response is to extend ActivityPub, one of the most popular and most discussed protocols of the Fediverse, with stronger authorization methods based on an object-capability model of computer security, allowing parties to retroactively withdraw consent from other parties to see or use their data. What is unique about the Fediverse is this both technical and cultural acknowledgement that openness has its limits, and is itself open to wide-ranging interpretations dependent on context, which are not fixed in time. This is a fundamentally new point of departure for reimagining social media today.

3. The Fediverse as a Site for Online Agonistic Pluralism

As we have established, one of the most important traits of the Fediverse is that the different software stacks and applications that constitute it can be hosted by virtually anyone and for any purpose. This means that it is possible to create an online community that can interface with the rest of the Fediverse but that operates according to its own local rules, guidelines, modes of organization, and ideology. In this process, each community is able to define itself not only through its own memetic language, interests, and scope, but also in relation to the other, via difference. Such specificity might make the Fediverse seem like an infrastructural assemblage that follows the principles of agonistic pluralism. Agonistic pluralism, or agonism, was first articulated by Ernesto Laclau and Chantal Mouffe, who then further developed this political theory. In Mouffe's view, political consensus is impossible and radical negativity cannot be avoided in a system where diversity is limited to similar competing groups within the same hegemonic order.[14] Mouffe's thesis addresses democratic systems where politics that fall outside of what the liberal consensus deems acceptable are systematically excluded. However, this process is also visible on corporate social media platforms, in the way they shape and control discourse in order to stay within the bounds of what is acceptable for the liberal paradigm, which is aligned with their own business interests. This has led to the radicalization of those who are excluded.

---

13   Around the time Gab joined the network, all Fediverse statistics jumped by approximately one million users. These numbers, like all Fediverse usage numbers, are contested. For context, see John Dougherty and Michael Edison Hayden, '"No Way" Gab has 800,000 Users, Web Host Says', *Southern Poverty Law Center*, 14 February 2019, https://www.splcenter.org/hatewatch/2019/02/14/no-way-gab-has-800000-users-web-host-says and emsenn (graden and unionize), Mastodon post, 10 August 2019, 04:51, https://tenforward.social/@emsenn/102590414178698570.

14   For an exhaustive introduction to Mouffe's writing, see Chantal Mouffe, *Agonistics: Thinking the World Politically*, London: Verso, 2013.

The bet made by agonism is that by creating a system in which a pluralism of hegemonies is permitted, it is possible to move from an understanding of the other as an enemy, to the other as a political adversary. For this to happen, different ideologies must be allowed to materialize via different channels and platforms. An important prerequisite is that the goal of political consensus must be abandoned and replaced with conflictual consensus, in which an acknowledgement of the other becomes the foundational building block of new relationships, even if this means, for example, accepting non-Western views on democracy, secularism, communities, and the individual. Translated to the Fediverse, it is clear that it already contains a relatively diverse political landscape and that transitions from political consensus to conflictual consensus can be witnessed in the way communities relate to one another. At the base of these conflictual exchanges are various points of view on the collective design and use of the software stack and the underlying protocols that would be needed to further enable a sort of online agonistic pluralism.

This said, the fact that discussions around the aforementioned usage of instance blocking and defederation are fiercely debated, and, at time of writing, with the seemingly irreconcilable presence of factions of radical left and alt-right in the Fediverse, the realities of antagonism will be highly challenging to resolve. The Fediverse's idea of a system in which different communities can find a place for themselves amongst others was concretely put to the test in July 2019, when the explicitly alt-right platform Gab announced it would change its code base, moving away from its proprietary system to instead rely on Mastodon's source code. As a project that explicitly takes a stance against the ideology of Gab, Mastodon was confronted with the neutrality of FLOSS licenses. Other Fediverse projects such as mobile phone clients FediLab and Tusky were also faced with the same issue; perhaps even more so, because the direct motivation for Gab's developers to switch to Fediverse software was to circumvent their ban from the Apple and Google app stores for violating their terms of service. By relying on generic FLOSS Fediverse clients, Gab would be able to escape such bans in the future, and also forge alliances with other ideologically compatible instances on the Fediverse.[15] As part of a larger anti-fascist strategy to de-platform and block Gab on the Fediverse, calls went out to software developers to add code that would prevent them from using their clients to log in to Gab servers. This resulted in extensive debates on the nature of FLOSS, the effectiveness of such measures on public source code modifications, given that they can be easily reverted, and on the political alignment of software maintainers.

At the heart of this conflict lies the question of the neutrality of the code, the network, and the protocols. Should – or even can – a client be neutral? Does doubling down on neutrality mean the maintainers condone alt-right ideology? What does it mean to block or to not block another instance? This latter question has created a complicated back-and-forth where some instances will demand other instances to explicitly take part in a conflict, by blocking specific other instances in order to avoid being blocked themselves. Neutrality, whether driven

---

15   Andrew Torba, 'Moving to the ActivityPub protocol as our base allows us to get into mobile App Stores without even having to submit and get approval of our own apps, whether Apple and Google like it or not', post to Gab, https://gab.com/a/posts/VnZRendFcDM1alBhNm9QeWV4d0xidz09, las accessed May 2019.

by ambivalence, unspoken support, hypocrisy, the desire to troll, a lack of interest, faith in apolitical technology, or by an agonistic desire to engage with all sides so as to reach a state of conflictual consensus, is very difficult to achieve. The Fediverse is the closest environment we currently have to a diverse global network of local singularities. However, its complex topology and struggle to deal with the infamous paradox of tolerance – what to do about the idea of free speech – shows the difficulty of reaching a state of conflictual consensus. It also demonstrates the challenge of translating a theory of agonism into a shared strategy for the design of protocols, software, and community guidelines. Tolerance and free speech have become volatile topics after nearly two decades of political manipulation and filtering within corporate social media; seeing how popular imageboards and discussion forums have failed to solve these issues does not make for a hopeful outlook for future experimentation.

Rather than reaching a state of agonistic pluralism, it could be that the Fediverse will create at best a form of bastard agonism through pillarization. That is to say, we could witness a situation in which instances would form large agonistic-without-agonism aggregations only among both ideologically and technically compatible communities and software, with only a minority of them able and willing to bridge with radically opposed systems. Regardless of the outcome, this question of agonism and of politics in general is crucial for net and computational culture. In the context of Western post-political systems and the way these are translated to the net, a sense of loss of political partisanship and agency has given the illusion, or delusion, that there is no longer a political compass. If the Fediverse teaches us anything, it is that the net and the FLOSS components of its infrastructure have never been more politicized than today. The politics that are generated and hosted on the Fediverse are not trivial but they are clearly articulated. What's more, as demonstrated by the proliferation of social media political celebrities and politicians actively using social media, a new form of representative democracy is emerging, in which the memetic language of post-digital cultures are effectively translated into the world of electoral politics and back.[16]

4. The Fediverse as a Shift from a Technical to a Social Understanding of Privacy

In the past, debates around the risks of corporate social media have focused on the issues of privacy and surveillance, especially since the Snowden revelations in 2013. Consequently, many of the technical responses, particularly those born out of FLOSS communities, have focused on addressing privacy through security. This was exemplified by the post-Snowden proliferation of specialized applications for secure encrypted messaging and email.[17] In these communities, the perceived threat is the possibility of surveillance at the network level, by either government agencies or large corporations. Proposed solutions are therefore conceived as tools that implement strong encryption of both the transmission and the content of messages, ideally making use of anonymity over

16   David Garcia, 'The Revenge of Folk Politics', transmediale/journal 1 (2018), https://transmediale.de/content/the-revenge-of-the-folk-politics.
17   hbsc & friends, 'Have You Considered the Alternative?', Homebrew Server Club, 9 March 2017, https://homebrewserver.club/have-you-considered-the-alternative.html.

peer-to-peer network topologies. These approaches, while thorough, require considerable technical knowledge on the part of users.

The Fediverse is then shifting from a predominantly technical to a more social understanding of privacy, as was clear in relation to discussions on issue trackers during the early stages of the development of Mastodon. The threat model discussed there is the one that consists of other users of the network, accidental associations between accounts, and the dynamics of online conversations themselves. This means that rather than focusing on technical features such as peer-to-peer topologies and end-to-end encryption, development has been centered around building robust moderation tools, granular visibility settings for posts, and the possibility to block other instances.

These features, which accommodate for a social understanding of privacy, have been developed and advocated for by members of marginalized communities, a substantial part of whom identify as queer. As Sarah Jamie Lewis notes:

> Much of the modern rhetoric around [. . .] privacy tools is focused on state surveillance. Queer communities often wish to hide things from some of their family and friends, while also being able to share parts of their life with others. Making friends, dating, escaping abusive situations, accessing healthcare, exploring themselves and others, finding jobs, engaging in safe sex work are all aspects of queer lives underserved by the modern privacy community.[18]

So while everyone has a stake in considering the privacy implications that come from (involuntary) associations between online accounts, for example between an employer and an employee, marginalized communities are disproportionately impacted by such forms of surveillance and their consequences. As the development of newer Fediverse platforms such as Mastodon got underway, with members of such communities helping to build them, these issues were put on the agenda of software development roadmaps. All of a sudden, tools that were used to track and discuss technical defects during the development of FLOSS also became a discursive venue for social, cultural, and political issues. We will return to this point in section six.

The techniques that were eventually developed included server-wide blocks, advanced moderation tools, content warnings, and improved accessibility. This allowed for geographically, culturally, and ideologically disparate communities to share the same network on their own terms. As such, the Fediverse can be understood as different communities that rally around a server, or instance, so as to create an environment where everyone feels comfortable. Again, this represents a third way: neither the model of privacy where technically inclined individuals are in full command of their own communications, nor the model whereby the multitude believes they have 'nothing to hide' simply because they have no say nor control over the systems they depend on. In effect, the move to a social understanding of privacy has

---

18   Sarah Jamie Lewis (ed), *Queer Privacy: Essays From The Margin Of Society,* Victoria, British Columbia: Lean Pub/Mascherari Press, 2017, p. 2.

shown that the Fediverse is now a working laboratory in which questions of social organization and governance can no longer pretend to be decoupled from software.

What matters is that the Fediverse represents a shift from defining the issues of surveillance and privacy as technical problems to defining them as social ones. However, the focus on social aspects of privacy has so far resulted in placing a lot of trust in other servers and administrators to act respectfully. This can be problematic, as for example direct messages, with their implied privacy, would be far better managed with technical solutions such as end-to-end encryption. Further, many of the solutions sought in Fediverse software development seem to be based on the collective rather than on the individual. This is not to say that technical security considerations are of no concern at all. Fediverse servers tend to come with 'privacy by default' settings, such as required transport encryption and the proxying of remote queries in order not to expose individual users. Still, this shift to a social understanding of privacy remains young, and the discussion must continue at many other levels.

5. The Fediverse as a Way Out of Data Sharecropping and Free Labor

Corporate social media platforms with their focus on self-gratifying metrics and gamification are infamous for taking free labor as far as they can. Whatever information is fed into the system, will be used to directly or indirectly create models, reports, and new datasets that have core economic value for the platform owners: enter the world of surveillance capitalism.[19]

So far regulating these products and services has been extremely difficult, in part because of effective lobbying from the platform owners and shareholders, but also, perhaps more importantly, because of the derivative nature of the monetization that takes place inside corporate social media. What is capitalized by these platforms is an algorithmic by-product, crude or not, of the activity and data uploaded by its users. This creates a distance that makes it ever-harder to grasp the relationship between online labor, user-generated content, tracking, and monetization. This distance effectively works in two ways. First, it obfuscates the exact mechanics at play, making it harder to regulate data capture and analysis. It allows for situations where these platforms can develop products that they can benefit from while still complying with privacy laws from different jurisdictions, and therefore promote their service as privacy friendly. The latter is often reinforced by giving their users all sorts of options to mislead them into believing they are in control of what they feed the machine. Second, by making it seem that no personally identifiable data is directly used for monetization; these platforms are hiding the economic transaction behind other types of transactions, such as personal interactions between users, professional opportunities, online community-managed groups and discussions, and so on. In the end, users are unable to make a connection between their social or professional activity and its exploitation because it is all derivative

---

19   Shoshana Zuboff, *The Age of Surveillance Capitalism: The Fight for a Human Future at the New Frontier of Power*, New York: PublicAffairs, 2019.

of other transactions that have become essential in our ever-connected lives, especially in the age of entreprecariat[20] and quasi-mandatory network connectivity.

As we saw in the discussion of how a social understanding of digital privacy informed the initial design of Mastodon, the Fediverse offers a refreshing take on the question of surveillance capitalism. Discussions surrounding user data and how these issues are tackled at the level of protocols and graphical interface design are quite transparent and open. These discussions take place publicly on the Fediverse and on related software project issue trackers. The way data circulates is made explicit to new users by other users or their local admin when they are welcomed onto an instance. These greetings usually contain information on how federation works and how that affects the visibility and access of the data they share.[21] This echoes what Robert Gehl sees as one of the characteristics of alternative social media platforms – that both the network and its code have a pedagogical function, demonstrating how they can be used, and how one can move beyond the habitual mode of limited user-permissions to take part in coding, administrating, and organizing such platforms.[22] In this sense, users are encouraged to become active in ways other than simply posting and liking, and are made aware of the ways in which their data circulate.

Yet regardless of how the community of an instance is organized, empowered, and actively participating in the platform and network – not to mention the fact that getting into coding is easier said than done – more control over data is not guaranteed. It is still possible to easily scrape or collect information from these platforms, possibly even more so than from corporate social networks since commercial services actively prevent others from exploiting their data silo. At present, it is quite simple to crawl the Fediverse and profile its users. Even though most Fediverse platforms are themselves against user tracking and data sharecropping, third parties can do so anyway because the Fediverse operates as an open network primarily designed for public posts. Additionally, as certain interests, notably political discussions, tend to be concentrated on specific servers, activist communities may be more readily exposed to intelligence. So while the Fediverse helps users to understand, or be reminded, that whatever is published online can and will escape their control, it cannot prevent all the habits and false sense of online security inherited from corporate social media from going on, after nearly two decades of digital privacy misinformation.[23]

Furthermore, although the exploitation of user labor is not the same as that on corporate social media platforms, there are still issues surrounding labor in this network. To understand these issues, we must first acknowledge the damage done by the free-to-use wonder of corporate social media on the one hand, and the misunderstanding of FLOSS practices on the other;

---

20   Silvio Lorusso, *Entreprecariat – Everyone Is an Entrepreneur. Nobody Is Safe*, Onomatopee: Eindhoven, 2019.
21   For an example of a frequently circulated user-generated introduction, see Noëlle Anthony, Joyeusenoelle/GuideToMastodon, 2019, https://github.com/joyeusenoelle/GuideToMastodon.
22   Throughout this text we use 'corporate social media' and 'alternative social media' as defined in Gehl, 'The Case for Alternative Social Media'.
23   For an ongoing survey of these issues, see Pervasive Labour Union Zine, https://ilu.servus.at.

namely, how labor issues and workers' struggles have been obfuscated in these processes.[24] This situation has led people to believe that software production, server maintenance, and online services should be available free of charge. Corporate social media platforms are able to financially support their infrastructure specifically because of the direct and indirect monetization of their users' content and activity. In a system where this monetization is avoided, impossible, or actively resisted, the problem of labor and exploitation surfaces at the level of server administration and software development, and concerns all those contributing to the design, consideration, and support of these infrastructures.

In response to this problem, there is a tendency in the Fediverse toward making the costs of operation of a community server explicit. Users and administrators alike encourage funding the various projects through donations, therefore acknowledging that the production and maintenance of these platforms cost money. More prominent projects such as Mastodon have access to larger funds and have set up a system through which contributors can get paid for their work.[25] These attempts to compensate labor are a good step, however making them more widespread, and maintaining such projects in the long run, will require more structural support. Without substantial funding for ongoing development and maintenance, these projects will remain contingent upon the exploitation of the free labor of well-meaning individuals, or subject to the whims of people making time for their FLOSS hobby. At the same time there is increasing acknowledgement and precedent that much of FLOSS can be considered public utility goods, which should be funded from public sources.[26] In times when the regulation of corporate social media is on the table for its role in eroding public institutions, the lack of public funding for non-predatory alternatives should be more actively discussed.

Finally, in some cases, non-technical tasks like moderation are remunerated by Fediverse communities. This raises the question of why some kinds of labor are compensated, and others not, if there is compensation at all. What about the vital early work of care and critique by members of marginalized communities in voicing how Fediverse projects should address a social understanding of privacy, for example? Without a doubt it was this work that enabled the Fediverse to reach the user base it has today. Then how can such work be measured? It happens in and throughout the network, in meta-discussion threads, or on issue trackers, which is not as quantifiable nor visible as code commits. So while there are some interesting shifts happening, it remains to be seen whether users and developers on the Fediverse can be made fully aware of these issues, and if economic models outside of surveillance capitalism can thrive to support non-exploitative solidarity and care across the whole stack.

24 Even though framed in the context of Tumblr, for a thorough discussion on the tension between digital labour, post-digital communities, and activism, see Cassius Adair and Lisa Nakamura, 'The Digital Afterlives of *This Bridge Called My Back:* Woman of Color Feminism, Digital Labor, and Networked Pedagogy', *American Literature* 89.2 (2017): 255-278.
25 'Mastodon', *Open Collective*, https://opencollective.com/mastodon.
26 For elements of discussion on the public funding of free software, as well as some analysis of early draft laws regarding the access of source code for software purchased with public money, see Jesús M. González-Barahona, Joaquín Seoane Pascual and Gregorio Robles, *Introduction to Free Software*, Barcelona: Universitat Oberta de Catalunya, 2009.

6. The Fediverse as the Rise of a New Kind of Usership

One way to understand the Fediverse is as a signifier of a set of practices, or rather a set of expectations and demands about social media software, in which the disparate efforts of alternative social media projects converge into a shared network with roughly aligned goals. Diverse models of usership, shared between servers, range from venture-capital-backed alt-right platforms to Japanese imageboard systems, anarcho-communist collectives, political factions, live-coding algoravers, 'safe spaces' for sex workers, gardening forums, personal blogs, and self-hosting cooperatives. These practices happen in parallel with the problem of data sharecropping and free labor, and represent part of the ongoing transformation of what it entails to be a software user.

The first software users, or users of computational devices, were also their programmers, and the ones who would then provide the tools and documentation for others to contribute actively to the development and usage of these systems.[27] This role was so important that the first user communities were fully supported and taken care of by hardware manufacturers. Fast forward a couple of decades and, with the growth of the computer industry, what it is to be a user has completely changed to a tamed consumer with limited opportunities to contribute or change the systems they use, beyond trivial or cosmetic customizations. It is this situation that helped shape much of the growing popularity of FLOSS in the 90s, as an adversary of proprietary commercial operating systems for personal computers, specifically reinforcing earlier concepts of users' freedom.[28] With the advent of Web 2.0, the situation changed again. Because of the communicative and ubiquitous dimension of the software behind corporate social media platforms, vendors have begun to offer a small window of opportunity to their users to give feedback, as a way to make their product more engaging and relevant to everyday activities. Users can usually easily report bugs, suggest new features, or help shape the platforms' culture through the conversations they have and content they share. Twitter is a well-known example of this, where core features such as the '@' usernames and the '#' hashtags were first suggested by users. Forums like Reddit also allow users to set up and moderate boards, creating distinct and specific communities.

On alternative social media platforms like the Fediverse, particularly in its early days, these forms of participation move a step further. Users do not only engage in bug reporting, or help with the creation of the products' culture, they also become involved with scrutinizing the code, debating its effects, and even contributing code back. As the Fediverse grows in size and encompasses a greater diversity of cultures and software stacks, the behaviors of this usership are becoming even more comprehensive. People set up additional nodes in the network and work on the development of tailored codes of conducts and terms of services that aid the enforcement of community guidelines for that node. They also consider how to make these efforts sustainable through funding via the community.

---

27 For instance, see Atsushi Akera, 'Voluntarism and the Fruits of Collaboration: The IBM UserGroup, Share', *Technology and Culture* 42.4 (2001): 710-736.
28 Sam Williams, *Free as in Freedom: Richard Stallman's Crusade for Free Software*, Farnham: O'Reilly, 2002.

This said, not all requests for change, including fully functional code contributions, are accepted by the main developers of the platforms. This is in part because the larger Fediverse platforms believe in well-considered default settings that work for diverse majorities, rather than the old archetypical model of FLOSS, to provide extensive customization and intricate options that appeal to programmers, but discourage many others. Thanks to the availability of source code, a rich ecosystem of modified versions of projects nevertheless exists, to extend, or limit, certain features while retaining a degree of compatibility with the wider network. Debates over the merits of features and the modified software they generate foster further discussion over the direction of such projects, which in turn leads to increased attention around their governance.

To be sure, these developments are neither new nor unique to the Fediverse. The way service facilitators are supported on the Fediverse, for example, is analogous to the way in which content creators on streaming platforms in gaming communities are supported by their audience. Calls for better governance of software projects are also ongoing in FLOSS communities more widely. The development of codes of conduct (a key document for Fediverse instances to lay out their vision of their community and politics) was introduced in various FLOSS communities in the early 10s, in response to systematic misogyny and the exclusion of minorities from FLOSS spaces both on- and offline.[29] Codes of conduct also serve the need for generative forms of conflict resolution across cultural and language barriers.

Likewise, many of the moderation and community management practices seen in the Fediverse have been informed by experiences on other platforms, by the successes and failures of other tools and systems. The synthesis and coordination of all these practices has become increasingly visible in the Fediverse. In turn, issues and approaches represented in the Fediverse set a precedent for other FLOSS projects, encouraging transformation and discussions that were until now limited or difficult to initiate.

It is obviously not the case, given the diversity of usership models, that the entirety of the Fediverse operates along these lines. The developments described above do though suggest how many models of usership are yet to be discovered and how the Fediverse is a productive environment for their trial. The evolving nature of usership on the Fediverse shows how much space there is between the stereotypical extremes of the surveillance capitalist model and the self-inflicted martyrdom of free-labor-powered platforms. This has implications for the role of users in relation to alternative social media, as well as for the development of FLOSS culture.[30]

---

29   Femke Snelting, 'Codes of Conduct: Transforming Shared Values into Daily Practice', in Cornelia Sollfrank (ed) *The Beautiful Warriors: Technofeminist Praxis in the 21st Century*, Colchester: Minor Compositions, 2019, pp. 57-72.
30   Dušan Barok, *Privatising Privacy: Trojan Horse in Free Open Source Distributed Social Platforms*, master thesis, Networked Media, Piet Zwart Institute, Rotterdam/Netherlands, 2011.

7. The Fediverse as the End of Free/Libre and Open Source Software as We Know It

Until now, the vast majority of discussions around FLOSS licensing have remained locked in a tiresome comparison between free software's emphasis on user ethics versus the open source approach based on economics.[31] Whether motivated by ethics or economics, both free software and open source software share the ideal that their position is superior to closed source and proprietary modes of production. However in both cases, the foundational liberal drive at the base of these ethical and economic perspectives is rarely challenged. This drive is deeply rooted in a Western context that over the past few decades has favored individual freedom in the form of liberalism and libertarianism at the expense of equality and care. Questioning this drive is a pivotal step, as this would open up discussions about other ways to approach the writing and circulation of, and access to, source code. By extension this would stop the pretension that these practices are either apolitical, universal, or neutral. Unfortunately, such discussions have been difficult to facilitate for reasons that go beyond the dogmatic nature of both free and open source software agendas. In fact they have been inconceivable because one of the most important aspects of FLOSS is that it was conceived as non-discriminatory in nature. To be sure, with non-discriminatory, we refer to FLOSS licensing, that permits anyone to make use of a FLOSS source code for any purpose.

There have been some efforts to try to tackle this problem, for example at the level of licensing – making discriminatory licenses to protect worker-owned productions, or to exclude use by the military and intelligence services.[32] These efforts were negatively received because of the non-discriminatory baseline of FLOSS and its discourse. To make things worse, the main concern of FLOSS advocacy has historically been about widespread adoption in administration, education, professional, and commercial environments, and depoliticization was seen to be key to achieving this goal. However more recently, the belief in, or the strategy of depoliticization has started to suffer in several ways.

First, the rise of this new kind of usership meant a new questioning of the archetypal models of governance of FLOSS projects, such as the benevolent dictator. Consequently, several long-standing FLOSS projects have been pressured to adopt accountability structures and migrate to community-oriented forms of governance such as co-ops or associations. Second, licenses now tend to be combined with other textual documents like copyright transfer agreements, terms of services, and codes of conduct. These documents are used to shape the community, make their ideological alignment clearer, and try to prevent manipulation and misunderstanding around vague notions like openness, transparency, and freedom. Third, the strong political coloring of source code challenges the existing understanding of

---

31 See the Stallman-Ghosh-Glott mail exchange on the FLOSS survey, 'Two Communities or Two Movements in One Community?', in Rishab Aiyer Ghosh, Ruediger Glott, Bernhard Krieger and Gregorio Robles, 'Free/Libre and Open Source Software: Survey and Study', FLOSS final report, International Institute of Infonomics, University of Maastricht, Netherlands, 2002, http://flossproject.merit.unu.edu/floss1/stallman.html.

32 For instance, see Felix von Leitner, 'Mon Jul 6 2015', *Fefes Blog*, 6 July 2015, https://blog.fefe.de/?ts=ab645846.

FLOSS. As previously mentioned, some of these efforts are driven by the desire to avoid the censorship and control of corporate social media platforms, while others explicitly seek to develop software for anti-fascist use. These efforts not only dispute the universality and global usefulness of large, general social media platforms, they also interrogate the supposed universality and neutrality of software. This is particularly true when software comes with politically explicit complementary terms, codes, and agreements for their users and developers to accept.

With its relatively diverse constituency of users, developers, agenda, software, and ideologies, the Fediverse is gradually becoming the most relevant system for the articulation of new forms of FLOSS critique. The Fediverse has become a site where traditional notions about FLOSS are confronted and revised by people who understand its use as part of a wider set of practices that challenge the status quo. Sometimes this happens in a reflective, discursive way across several communities, sometimes through the materialization of experiments and projects that directly challenge FLOSS as we know it. It has become the sprawling site where constructive critiques of FLOSS and a longing for its reimagination are most vivid. In its current state, FLOSS culture feels like a patched-up collection of irreconcilable pieces from another era, and it is urgent to revaluate many of its characteristics that have been taken for granted. If we can accept the much-needed sacrilege of thinking of free software without free software, it remains to be seen what could fill the void left by its absence.

AUTHOR BIOGRAPHIES

AUTHOR BIOGRAPHIES

CLEMENS APPRICH

Clemens Apprich is assistant professor in media studies at the University of Groningen and permanent fellow at the Centre for Digital Cultures at Leuphana University of Lüneburg, where he is one of the editors of *spheres*, an open peer-reviewed journal for digital cultures. He is an affiliate of the Digital Democracies Group at Simon Fraser University, Canada; the Global Emergent Media Lab at Concordia University, Montreal; and the Brandenburg Centre for Media Studies at the University of Potsdam. His current research deals with filter algorithms and their application in data analysis as well as machine learning methods. Apprich is the author of *Technotopia: A Media Genealogy of Net Cultures* (Rowman & Littlefield International, 2017), and, together with Wendy Chun, Hito Steyerl, and Florian Cramer, co-authored *Pattern Discrimination* (University of Minnesota Press/meson press, 2019).

JOHANNA BRUCKNER

Johanna Bruckner is an artist, with recent solo exhibitions and performances at Kunstraum Niederösterreich, Vienna, the Centre d'Art Contemporain Genève, and Migros Museum für Gegenwartskunst, Zurich. Group shows include at Haus der Kulturen der Welt and KW Institute for Contemporary Art in Berlin, and the 57th Venice Biennale. She is currently an artist-in-residence at the Swiss Institute in Rome.

DAPHNE DRAGONA

Daphne Dragona is a curator and writer based in Berlin. She was part of the curatorial team of transmediale from 2015 until 2019, with a focus on the conference and workshop program. Her work engages with artistic practices and methodologies that question contemporary forms of power. Her topics of interest include: the controversies of connectivity, the promises of the commons, the challenges of artistic subversion, the instrumentalization of play, care and empathy, and the potential of kin-making technologies in the time of climate crisis. She has curated exhibitions at Onassis Stegi and the National Museum of Contemporary Art in Athens; LABoral, Gijón; Aksioma, Ljubljana; Alta Technología Andina, Lima; and Le Lieu unique, Nantes. Her articles have been published in books, journals, magazines, and exhibition catalogs by Springer, Sternberg Press, and Leonardo Electronic Almanac, among others. She holds a PhD from the Faculty of Communication and Media Studies, University of Athens.

KRISTOFFER GANSING

Kristoffer Gansing is a curator, writer, and researcher living in Berlin, where between 2011 and 2020 he has been the artistic director of nine editions of transmediale. Intersecting art, theory, and technology, Gansing's writing and curation has a post-digital outlook, where digitalization has become part of everyday life. His PhD 'Transversal Media Practices' dealt with how media-archaeological art practices reconfigure linear conceptions of technological development, and was published by Malmö University Press in 2013. He co-edited *across & beyond: A transmediale Reader on Post-digital Practices, Concepts, and Institutions*, with Ryan Bishop, Jussi Parikka, and Elvia Wilk (Sternberg Press, 2016). Gansing previously worked with the artist-run TV channel *tv-tv* in Copenhagen, and as co-director of the media art festival The Art of the Overhead, devoted to the near-forgotten medium of the overhead projector.

LORENA JUAN

In her curatorial practice, Lorena Juan works with experimental formats, public space, and collaboration in the frame of queer feminist collectivities. Her most recent projects were presented at Kunstraum Kreuzberg/Bethanien ('Capitalo, Chthulu, and a Much Hotter Compost Pile', 2018), nGbK neue Gesellschaft für bildende Kunst ('Lucky', 2018), and Schwules Museum* ('Extra+Terrestrial', 2019) in Berlin. In 2019, she was part of the jury for the research stipends for artists and curators of the Berliner Senat and curator-in-residence at Rupert, Vilnius. Juan is part of the curatorial working group for 'Kunst im Untergrund 2020/2021', organized by nGbK. She is the co-founder and curatorial lead of the queer feminist collective and online platform COVEN BERLIN.

AAY LIPAROTO

Multidisciplinary artist Aay Liparoto uses long-term performance as a form of research to examine the power of the banal. Their output is mainly in video, text, and performance, working with accessible technology, personal digital archives, and DIY strategies to reflect on the mechanics of everyday life. In their solo and collaborative practice they are focused on feminist co-authorship as a method for resisting the over-simplification of narratives around historically marginalized voices.

GEERT LOVINK

Geert Lovink is a Dutch media theorist, internet critic, and author of Uncanny Networks (2002), Dark Fiber (2002), My First Recession (2003), Zero Comments (2007), Networks Without a Cause (2012), Social Media Abyss (2016), Organization after Social Media (with Ned Rossiter, 2018), and Sad by Design (2019). He founded the Institute of Network Cultures at Amsterdam University of Applied Sciences in 2014. The institute organizes conferences, publications, and research networks such as Video Vortex: Moving Image Beyond YouTube, Society of the Query: Web Search and Search Engines, Unlike Us (alternative social media), Critical Point of View (Wikipedia), and MoneyLab (digital economy in the arts).

ALESSANDRO LUDOVICO

Alessandro Ludovico is a researcher and artist, editor-in-chief of *Neural* magazine since 1993. He received his PhD in English and media from Anglia Ruskin University, Cambridge (UK). He is associate professor at the Winchester School of Art, University of Southampton. Ludovico has published and edited several books, and has lectured internationally. With Paolo Cirio he co-authored the award-winning 'Hacking Monopolism Trilogy' of artworks (*Google Will Eat Itself*, *Amazon Noir*, *Face to Facebook*). http://neural.it.

AYMERIC MANSOUX

Aymeric Mansoux has been messing around with computers and networks for far too long. He was a founding member of server-based collective GOTO10 (*FLOSS+Art* anthology, Puredyne distro, make art festival). Recent collaborations include: *The SKOR Codex*, an archive about the impossibility of archiving; *What Remains*, an 8-bit video game about the manipulation of public opinion and whistleblowing for the 1985 Nintendo Entertainment System; and LURK, a server infrastructure for discussions around cultural freedom, new media art, and net culture. Aymeric received his PhD from the Centre for Cultural Studies, Goldsmiths, University of London in 2017, for his investigation of the decay of cultural diversity and techno-legal forms of social organization within free and open-source cultural practices. He currently runs the Experimental Publishing (XPUB) master course at the Piet Zwart Institute, Rotterdam. https://bleu255.com/~aymeric.

RACHEL O'DWYER

Rachel O'Dwyer is a lecturer in digital cultures at the National College of Art and Design, Dublin. She was formerly a research fellow at Connect – Centre for Future Networks and Communications at Trinity College Dublin, and a Fulbright scholar in collaboration with the Future of Money project at the University of California, Irvine. Her research focuses on the intersection of cultural and digital economies, in particular networks and digital payments, surveillance capitalism and its resistance. She is curator of the Dublin Art and Technology Association and co-editor of *Neural* magazine. She has had articles published by *London Review of Books*, *Journal of Cultural Economy*, *Convergence: The International Journal of Research into New Media Technologies*, *Neural*, *Longreads*, the Institute of Network Cultures, and MIT Press.

LUIZA PRADO DE O. MARTINS

Luiza Prado de O. Martins is an artist and researcher whose work engages with material and visual cultures through decolonial and queer theories. She is particularly interested in technologies of birth control and their entanglements with the colonial hierarchies of gender, race, ethnicity, class, and nationality. Her current research project, 'A Topography of Excesses', examines the transmission of Indigenous and folk knowledges of herbal birth control in Brazil as a decolonizing practice of radical care.

ROEL ROSCAM ABBING

Roel Roscam Abbing is an artist and researcher whose work deals with the issues and cultures surrounding networked computation. He engages with themes such as network infrastructures, the politics of technology, and DIY approaches. He is a doctoral candidate in interaction design at Malmö University.

FEMKE SNELTING

Femke Snelting works as an artist and designer, developing projects at the intersection of design, feminism, and free software. She explores how digital tools and practices might co-construct each other. She has been a member of Constant, a nonprofit, artist-run association for art and media based in Brussels since 2003.

FLORIAN WÜST

Florian Wüst has been the film and video curator of transmediale since 2016. As an artist, film curator, and publisher he deals with social and economic progress in modernity as well as with urban political issues. He has curated film programs for international art institutions, cinemas, and festivals. Wüst is co-editor of the DVD *The Modern City. Film essays on the new urbanity of the 1950s and 60s* (2015), and co-founder of the journal series *Berlin Journals—On the History and Present State of the City*.

www.ingramcontent.com/pod-product-compliance
Lightning Source LLC
Chambersburg PA
CBHW052321220526
45472CB00001B/210